How To Hear God:
He Still Speaks

By Pastor Dr. Jomo Cousins

Dr. Jomo Cousins

Senior Pastor, Love First Christian Center

Printed 2022

ISBN Number: 9798355900540

Love First Christian Center
℅ Dr. Jomo Cousins, Senior Pastor
12847 Balm Riverview Drive
Riverview, FL 33579
info@lovefirstchristiancenter.com

TABLE OF CONTENTS

Introduction

To my faithful followers who have joined me on my writing journey from *Fully Equipped: God's Total Package* to *ABC's of Success: Surviving the Storms*, then *Prayer Life: The Conversation to Watch Your Mouth The Workbook*, and most recently, *60 Prayers in 60 Seconds: Strictly Business*, I say, thank you and welcome back!

For my new readers, I want to extend a warm welcome to you, as well. My journey is far from over; I've got plenty more to teach. Stay connected. Laugh, learn, and grow with me. These may be my words, but they're your message, and I want you to receive every one God wants you to have.

I believe that a person's most important relationship is their relationship with God. When I wrote *Prayer Life: The Conversation*, my goal was to show you how to have a meaningful and growing relationship with God through consistent prayer. This book, *How to Hear God: He Still Speaks*, is a continuation of that thought process. Prayer is simply defined as you talking to God and allowing God to talk to you. Many people have struggled with understanding how God speaks and how He communicates with us. In this book, I will try to help you understand some of the methods He uses.

I want to thank my awesome wife, Charmaine, and my three incredible children, Jomo, Jamya, and Josiah. You guys are a gift to me. I want to thank the faithful members of Love First Christian Center who have followed me on this journey and all those who have followed me on Facebook, YouTube, Twitter, and my morning prayer line.

I'd also like to thank my writing team who helped me, Melanie Lynch, Loretha Green, Phaaedra McKesson, and Omar Richardson.

Chapter One

Do You Hear What I Hear?

Do you hear what I hear?

Do you hear Me now?

Do you hear Me now?

Do you hear Me now?

Now, I have a question I want to ask you.

If God wrote you a personal letter every day, would you read it?

I'm going to ask you the question again:

If God, The Almighty God, wrote you a letter every day, would you read it? Would you find the time to read a personal letter from an all-knowing, all-seeing, ever-loving Source who told you in advance that He would make "all things work together for [your] good?" Would you want to know what the sole Creator of the Heavens and Earth had to say about *your* day? For most people, this might seem impossible, but the truth is God is always trying to speak to us. The real question is, why don't we always hear Him?

Here's our challenge: we spend six days a week focusing on family, work, health, finances, and all of life's other demands. Then, on Sunday, we think that if we go to church—brick and mortar *or* bedside—God should show up and quickly show out before lunch or the game (preferably both) so that we can have the rest of our day to do as we please. I mean, that's not *too much* to ask of a God who parted a whole sea and created a living man out of clay, *right*? Surely that same God could straighten out our issues in a five-minute conversation, *right?* The short answer is yes, He could, but with God, as with anything else, what you put in is what you will get out. God is no exception. He is a God of order and a God of process. If we don't put enough time into the *process* of connecting with Him through reading His Word, we cannot get all the benefits of His wisdom and guidance.

I want you to begin to see the Bible as more than just a Christian book of speeches and stories; see it as God's personal language and vocabulary. The more we interact with it, the more we begin to understand it—especially if we have someone helping to translate it for us. That's what the Holy Spirit does. He clarifies scripture and helps us become well-versed and more fluent in God's language, God's ways, and, ultimately, God's will for our lives. Don't miss out on what God wants you to know. Rest assured; God is always speaking to you.

Do you hear Me now?

Do you hear Me?

Do you?

What do many of us do when we can't hear from God as often as we'd like? When we feel like God is turning a deaf ear to our needs? We treat Him like a post office with special delivery options!

Some of us attend church on Sundays, specifically looking for **Priority Express Mail Service** from God. We say, "Lord, I need a blessing *now*! Do it *now*, Jesus! I'm even willing to pay extra for it!" In other words, we try to turn an **on-time God** into an **on-demand God**. We hurry God along, expecting faster delivery of His wisdom, word, and presence so we can return to the busyness of our hectic schedules.

For others who might not want to get up early for a long Sunday morning sermon, we go to Bible Study during the week for **First Class Mail Service** instead. It's not as fast as Priority Express, so our package (or message) might take a little longer in the week to reach us, but we're okay with that because we'd rather pay less in "sleep equity" to get our package on Wednesday evening instead of Sunday morning.

Meanwhile, God has a word waiting for us on Monday, Tuesday, Thursday, Friday, and Saturday, too! I'm not minimizing the importance of Sunday services or Bible studies, but I want you to understand that **God speaks every day**!

Often, we get off course during the week because we're not

getting fed a daily word. So, we become malnourished. Then we show up on Sundays starving for a word to revive and sustain us. We become so desperate that we approach God with a "right now" spirit. We need Express Mail or, at the very least, Priority Mail!

God tries to tell us many things, but most of us have a whole bunch of unopened mail from Him stacked up. Important, personal messages that have insight, ideas, and answers specifically for us just piled up, unchecked, and unused.

Has anybody ever neglected to pay a bill because you didn't open a letter? Truth be told, when I didn't have the money, I didn't *want* to open the letter, but by not opening it, I could have missed out on good news, too!

As a pastor and a business owner, I get a lot of mail. I once found a letter in my office with a check in it. I had the letter so long that the check had expired! I wonder how many checks you missed by not checking your mail. I wonder how many appointments you missed by not being where God wanted you to be because you simply didn't read your daily mail.

Do you hear what I hear?

Hear this clearly: **Malachi 3:6 (NKJV)** says, ***"For I am the Lord, I do not change."*** If God spoke to Adam and Eve in Genesis, don't you think He *still* wants to talk to you?

And look at what **Hebrews 13:8 (AMP)** says about Jesus: ***"Jesus Christ is [eternally changeless, always] the same yesterday and today and forever."***

If God has not changed and Jesus does not change, then that also means their delivery systems have not changed. So, it's not a question of whether God delivers. The true question is, are we available when their deliveries are made?

Look at what **Psalm 81:8 (AMP)** says: ***"Hear, O my people, and I will admonish you..."*** Admonish means to advise or give wisdom. ***"I will admonish you – O Israel, if you would listen to me!"***

God's asking the children of Israel to listen to Him. We have to assume God wants to tell them (and us) something He was speaking about.

Psalms 81:9 (AMP): *"Let there be no strange god among you, or shall you worship any foreign god."*

In this verse, I believe God was trying to warn us not to allow different voices to speak into our lives. If we're not careful, those voices could become gods.

"Pastor, what do you mean by "gods?"

A god (with a little "g") is something that we give so much time, money, and attention to that we make it a priority in our lives over God. Be it a person, a TV show, a car, or even a goal; we can all think of something that has become so important to us that it distracts us from building a stronger relationship with God; that is something that He would consider an idol or a "god."

You can determine what you have turned into a "god" in your life by checking these three areas:

Area One: Time Allocation. Where you put your time is a great indicator of what you consider a god. I know during football season, I spend some extra hours watching games; for others, it may be some other programs. Well, if you know more about *players* than *prayers* and more *statistics* than *scriptures*, you might want to revisit your holy playbook and rethink your life's game plan.

Area Two: Talent Utilization. How much of your gifting are you allowing God to use? Just write it down and start looking at your totals. Make two columns and start listing your God-given gifts in one column. In the other column, write how you use each gift to glorify God or help build His kingdom. If you see more gaps in one column than the other, that will tell you if you have or haven't been making what's important to God important to you.

Area Three: Money Distribution. All we have to do is go through your bank statements to determine where your "gods" lie. **Matthew 6:21** says, *"Where your treasure is, there will your heart be also!"*

So, take some time to examine your time allocation, talent utilization, and money distribution. You will realize quickly which God or gods reign over your life.

Seriously though, God says that we should not have any alternative gods so that we can keep a proper balance in our lives. I love football and basketball, but once I see that they take too much time from my praying, studying, or attending church, I know they have become out of balance. There's nothing wrong with liking any of them, but we must be careful not to turn them into idols. Otherwise, before we know it, we'll make choices based on things instead of God.

Back to **Psalms 81**
Psalm 81:10 (NKJV): *"I am the Lord your God, Who brought you*

out from the land of Egypt; Open your mouth wide, and I will fill it."

God tries to remind the people of Israel about where He brought them from and what He brought them through so that they would listen to Him and continue to have victory over their adversaries with His help. He said, *"...open your mouth wide and I will fill it."* God not only wants to help us win, but He wants to supply our needs, too. He said you shouldn't just open your mouth a little bit. Open your mouth wide because He wants to fill it with whatever we need! The challenge is, will we listen to Him?

In **John 10:27 (AMP)**, the Lord says, *"The sheep that are My own hear My voice and listen to Me; I know them, and they follow Me."*

Now, notice He says *"My own"* and "*My voice*," meaning some sheep are listening to another voice. Listen to me *carefully:* you are where you are in life based on **the voices you heed** and **the choices you make**. I'll repeat it – **you are where you are in life based on the voices you heed and the choices you make.**

Okay, let me say it another way through a funny story. If you've ever been in a fight, you can relate.

I remember this young brother. Micky was his name. I don't know if that was his real name or a nickname; I just knew everyone called him Micky. Micky was probably about 6' 6" or

6' 7". He had an afro, and I had dreads. He liked to play basketball, but he was not good. I, on the other hand, was not great, but I was better than good.

Anyway, students would play pick-up games during lunch hour. At the time, I was dunking on people. One day, Micky decided he was going to block my shot. I just loved when people wanted to block my shots because that's when I could really get the good dunks in! Well, right after I dunked on him, I kind of said something smart because that's what I usually do. After I said what I said, Micky went and got the broom from the school's janitor and swung it at me! He missed, but I knew things wouldn't end there.

I think most people have a pretty good sense of when something is about to go wrong! My friend said, *"Jomo, you know you're going to have to fight Micky before the week's out, right?"* I knew it was coming, but I just didn't want to admit it. It was just a matter of time. Later, at home, my friends and I started shadowboxing. I had to get myself prepared for the inevitable!

There are some days when you're just going to *have* to fight. You don't *want* to fight, but some fights just come to you!

A few days later, I was standing in front of Mr. Samuda's class; he was my Spanish teacher. He was also our school's Athletic Director. I had my foot on the wall conversing with a young lady. This was pre-Jesus! Suddenly, I see Micky coming around the corner from the end of the hall.

Usually, your antennas go up when you know you're about to fight! I saw him coming around the corner, and he had *that look*. If you don't know the fight look, it's kind of a smirk, but it's not a smile. The person walks towards you with their head cocked to one side. When I saw Micky coming at me like that, I said, *"Okay, let me pay attention!"*

In one moment, I was talking to the lady. Then, next thing you know, I could hear myself shout out, *"dang!"* He caught me! Micky sucker-punched me! Now I was a world-class wrestler (in my head), you know. If anybody grew up in my time, we all watched WWF matches (now WWE) on TV. As soon as I felt the punch, I grabbed him by the legs and body-slammed him! My friends said all they saw were Micky's legs *flying* through the air. Once I got him on the ground, I just kept hitting him until Mr. Samuda came and got me off him.

Mr. Samuda took me to the office and said, *"Jomo, I can't believe you're fighting in school! Why didn't you come tell us?"* I never understood that! Who's going to go tell a teacher, *"Hey, sir! I don't know if I will get whooped today, but there's a high probability that a beatdown will go down! I don't know where it's going to happen; I just know I need to be ready."* I said, *"That doesn't make any sense! How am I supposed to tell you when a fight will happen? When you get hit, you just respond!"*

What does this have to do with the message in **John 10:27** about God's sheep hearing His voice?

The voice told me to get ready; the voice told me to look up, that he was coming around the corner. But I was preoccupied with that young lady and I chose not to listen to the voice. Instead, I continued to *conversate with* that young lady, so I got caught with a punch to the head. I was lucky to recover from that, but God was trying to give me a heads-up. How many times in your life did the voice try to save you, but you decided to do something different anyway?

Life is all about voices and choices.

My friends Omar and Derrick and I used to walk to school together every day. Derrick had said to me, "*You know you have to fight him, right?*" Omar had said, *"Let's shadow box so you can be ready!"* My friends thought they were doing the right thing by gearing me up to fight, but when I look back over my mistake—because, you know, I got suspended and all the other stuff—it was the voices I heeded and the choices I made that got me into that mess. Truth be told, most of the time, when we get caught up, it's because we are listening to everything else *but* the voice of God.

We've all heard those voices saying the wrong things at the wrong times!

"You're not going to let them talk to you like that, are you? You better do something about it..."

These types of people are called "jumper cables." Just like jumper cables can start up a car, these kinds of people can push you to do something you should not do. They're around you when you say things like:

"You know what? I'm going to work on my marriage!"
"I'm going to work on myself."
"I'm going to go back to school and finish."

Jumper cable people respond with, "Why are you going to do that?

Jumper cable people are people who will discourage you from doing the right things in the eyes of God and man.

So, we must be mindful when we find ourselves in bad spots. It was the voices we heeded and the choices we made. Your life is based on three things: choices, decisions, and consequences. We should spend most of our time analyzing the consequences of our actions. With the process, we give God time to speak to us with discernment.

"Now, Pastor, how do I know it's God's voice?"

Well, God is not going to say, *"Put sugar in their tank."*

God's not going to say, *"Put their car on bricks."*

God is not going to say, *"Cut them."* That's not God.

God will not go against His character, for He is love. He says, *"Love your neighbor (Matthew 22:39)*." He says, *"Forgive them for they know not what they do (Luke 23:34)."* That's God. So, you have to fight that urge of your flesh because the flesh says, *"You cut me, I cut you...you cuss me, I cuss you*," and you've got to fight that flesh because the flesh is real. The flesh loves to lash out and sin.

Let's get back into Psalms 81. Look what it says in verse 11: *"...but my people will not listen to my voice, and Israel did not consent to obey me. So I gave them up to the stubbornness of their own heart to walk in the path of their own counsel."*

Get away from people who have your problem. Get around people who have your answer.

I'm going to say it another way: get away from people who have your weakness and get around people that have strengths you desire. Weakness will enable more weakness. Get away from that. Why? Because they will make you feel comfortable in your sinful nature(issue). That's why you see those with similar issues often hang together because nobody will hold them accountable to improve and grow.

Okay, let me take you back real quick. Do you remember the time before Caller ID? When the phone rang, but you couldn't identify who was calling? This story is for those forty and above.

Once you answered the phone, you knew the voice, and no one had to tell you who it was.

How could we discern their voice with no Caller ID? It's because we had a relationship with the person, and we spoke to them long enough that we could identify their voice. Our ability to hear God's voice is based on the time we invest with Him. The more time we spend with Him, the greater our ability will be to discern His voice.

We must change our interaction with God from only being when we come to church to when we get up in the morning and throughout our days. We must open our daily mail from God because overnight mail costs too much and wastes valuable time. It's so much cheaper just to listen. Every day, God has a message for you, but we must avail ourselves to receive it.

I ask you the question again, if God wrote you a letter every day, how long would it take for you to read it?

You must grow and be able to position yourself to where, every day, you get some word in you and give God time to speak to you. For those who may not know, I've been praying to and for the masses consistently every morning for over a decade now, and I believe it's a part of my purpose. I got word from God that this is a part of the assignment He gave me.

I was at a point in my life where I was trying to figure out my direction, and in that season, I decided to tell God that I would commit to praying every day. Within the first week, I had already overslept one day. I went to the bathroom, and when I turned the light on, I heard an audible voice say, "Where were you?" I knew I was home alone. Still, the voice was there, and I could not deny what I had heard. I was instantly convicted. And since that day until now, I have been diligent in seeking God daily in prayer. To be clear, God doesn't audibly speak that often in this journey called life but uses many forms of communication to give us instruction. The purpose of this book is to give you an understanding of the different ways He communicates with His children.

When I started on my prayer journey, my prayers were not as long and strong as they currently are. My prayers grew based on my relationship with God growing. I would pray using God's word and for God's will to be revealed (which is God's perfect plan for your life). As my biblical knowledge grew, so did the length and intensity of my prayers. The greater our relationship is with God, the greater our obedience should be to His word. So, when people say, "Pastor, I don't know how to pray," I know that's no excuse for *not learning* how to pray.

I remember a time when I was wrestling with how much I should give for one of our annual giving days. I told God I was going to give $10,000. So, as I was in a car line waiting to pick up my kids, I started negotiating with God. Does anybody negotiate with God? Come on, let's be honest. So, I started negotiating with God. I said, **"Lord, when I give $10,000, you don't expect me to tithe too, do you?"** And God said, "*You told* me at the beginning of the year, 'Lord, I'm going over and beyond this year.' And then God said, *"Jomo, remember what you said?"* And I responded, *"I did say that, didn't I?"*

Guess what, family? We all wrestle with obeying God's voice. Your wrestling might be different from mine. God tells you to go over there and help that person, and you struggle to do it, saying, **"Lord, they are nasty and rude."** Well, could it be that God put you in that position because that was your assignment, but you won't listen because you can't get past your feelings? Feelings, nothing more than feelings; stop catching them.

Let's get back to Psalms 81
Psalms 81:13, let me say it again: *"Oh that my people would listen to me, that usually walk in my ways."*

Psalms 37:23, look what it says here, oh this is good: *"The Lord directs the steps of the godly he delights in every detail..."*
"Pastor, why is this critical?" You need to know that God cares about small matters, too. You don't have to wait for the big stuff to call on Him; you can call on Him for every detail.

Let's get back to Psalms 81
Psalms 81

[11] *"But My people would <u>not listen to My voice</u>, and Israel <u>did not [consent to] obey Me</u>. [12] "So I gave them up to the stubbornness of their heart, to walk in [the path of] their own counsel. [13] "<u>Oh, that My people would listen to Me</u>, that Israel*

would walk in My ways! [14] *"Then I would quickly subdue and humble their enemies and turn My hand against their adversaries;* [15] *Those who hate the Lord would pretend obedience to Him and cringe before Him, and their time of punishment would be forever.* [16] *"But I would feed Israel with the finest of the wheat; and with honey from the rock I would satisfy you."*

Five Benefits of Obedience to God's Voice in Psalms 81. Look what happens:

1. God will subdue your enemies.
2. God will turn His hand against your adversaries. You're not going to fight your own battles anymore. God will fight them for you.
3. You will be blessed eternally.
4. God provides the best things. Notice He says the "finest wheat, the best honey." Why would you settle for anything less if God will give you the best?
5. God will satisfy you with good things.

Wisdom Key: Just Listen

"Now, therefore, my son, listen to me, pay attention to the words of my mouth." Proverbs 7:24

In this scripture, that's all He's asking us to do. Here are 10 Keys to Hearing from God

10 Keys to Hearing from God

1. **Ask** – James 4:2-3, Matthew 7:7-9 You have not because you ask not.
2. **Have Faith** - Hebrews 11:6 It's impossible to please Him without it.
3. **Listen** - Psalms 37:23 The steps of a good man are ordered by God.
4. **Shut up** - James 1:19 Be quick to listen and slow to speak.
5. **Relationship order** - Matthew 6:33 God must be a priority.
6. **Spend time in scriptures** - John 1:1-14 Jesus and the word are one.
7. **Confirm** - Mark 16:20 God always backs up His word.
8. **Write it Down** - Hab. 2:2 Write down what God gives you.
9. **Location** - Psalms 16:11 Proximity helps with frequency.
10. **Listen to your conscience** - Romans 9:1 Our conscience is our receiver to God

I close with this letter from God to you:

Good morning. As you got up, I watched and hoped you would talk to me, just a few words, such as 'thank you' to me for something good in your life. Yesterday or last week would do, but I noticed you were busy selecting the right clothes for work. I waited to hear from you again when you ran around the house collecting papers. I knew there'd be a few minutes to stop and say hello, but you never slowed down. I wanted to tell you that

I could help you accomplish more today than yesterday if you could just give me a little bit of time. At one point, you waited 15 minutes in the chair with nothing to do. I waited to hear from you then I saw you spring to your feet. I thought you wanted to talk to me, but you ran to the phone and called your friend. I watched as off to work you went, and I patiently waited all day long to hear from you. With all your activities, you're too busy to talk to me.

I noticed you looked around at lunch. Maybe you felt embarrassed to talk to me. You glanced at three tables over and noticed some of your friends were talking to me, but you wouldn't. There was still more time left than I hoped that we would talk. You went home, and you had many things to do. After you were done, you turned on the TV. Just about anything goes there, and you spent many hours watching. I waited as you continued to watch TV and eat your meal, but again you wouldn't talk to me.

At bedtime, you were totally tired. After you said goodnight to your family, you plopped into bed and fell asleep. I had so much I wanted to be a part of your day. We could have done so much more and had so much fun together. I love you so much that I wait every day for a thought, a prayer, or thanks. Well, maybe tomorrow. I'll be waiting.

Your friend, God.

Question: How much time does it take to talk to God? "Morning Lord. Thank you, Jesus." The more time you give God to speak to you, the greater the conversation is. We have a responsibility to speak to God, but we have a greater responsibility to allow God to speak to us.

We all do what's important to us and make time for what's important to us.

Question: If someone said they loved you but never made time for you, would you believe them?

Question: How do you think God feels about your relationship with Him? Do you only talk to Him when you need Him?

Simple Ways to Talk to God
- Hello, Lord; thank you for life, breath, and strength.
- Thank you, Father God, thank you for all your blessings.
- Thank you for my job.
- Thank you for my kids.
- Thank you for the home I'm in.
- Is there something I need to know?
- Is there something you want me to do?

Whatever way God communicates to you, learn that voice well. As our relationship with God grows, so do the ways in which He communicates. As babies, God will communicate to us in grand ways. As our relationship with Him grows, we will pick up the subtle ways in which He communicates with us.

Questions

1. Do you think you give God enough time to speak to you?

2. How could you make more time for God?

3. What are the other gods of your lifetime?

4. What are the main distractions that you need to remove?

5. Can you remember a time when you missed God's voice, and it didn't work out well for you?

6. Can you remember a time when you heard God's voice and were blessed?

7. Who are the main voices in your life?

8. Who are the jumper cable people in your life?

9. Who is your trusted source for wisdom and insight?

10. Have you ever made a commitment to God and didn't follow through?

Chapter Two

Man On the Run

I have always loved movies with lots of action and people trying to escape something. When I was younger, I would watch shows like *The A-Team* and *MacGyver*, and now I watch the *Jason Bourne* movies repeatedly. It's just something about people running for their lives that moves me.

From the beginning of time, man has been running and hiding from God, as Adam hid from God in the garden. In the book of Jonah, you will see a man on the run. The story of Jonah is going to be our object lesson on how God tries to communicate with us.

In this story, we will see how God used a progressive form of communication in dealing with him. Whether you believe it or not, God wants a relationship with us where He can speak to us one on one and where we can receive guidance. We know this is true from Genesis, where it speaks of God having daily conversations with Adam.

As we go through the book of Jonah, I will show you the four levels that God tried to connect with him and how it can benefit us. These four P's will change your life forever.

Level 1 - Personally

God always starts by trying to speak to us personally, and when that is not received;

Level 2 - A Person

Then God will try to speak to us through a person, and when that is not received;

Level 3 - Problem

God will try to speak to us through a problem, and when that is not received;

Level 4 - Pain

God will try to speak to us through pain. I learned in my life that change often doesn't come until pain sets in.

God's preferred method of growing us is through a mentorship program with Him and others He has sent into our lives. But if we choose not to receive the messages from our mentors, we best believe God has a plan. And that plan will involve a Tormentor. You will notice the difference in the words mentor and tormentor; the –tor, which is the root word of "tornado." A tornado turns things around and moves them to another place. God will use a tormentor to turn you around and move you to another place.

But we can choose to be willing and obedient and not go through some of the problems and pains that He sends our way to turn us back to Him, which is where we get the word "repent."

Let's get into our text, from the book of Jonah.

Jonah 1 (AMP)

¹ Now the word of the Lᴏʀᴅ came to Jonah the son of Amittai, saying, ² "Go to Nineveh, that great city, and proclaim [judgment] against it, for their wickedness has come up before Me."

Level 1 - Personally

In this text, we see God makes a clear command to Jonah. In the command, God gives the location he is supposed to go, the job assignment, and the message he is supposed to deliver. God doesn't care about your opinion of His plan; He just wants it done. I believe we think that God's instructions are like the messages from *Mission Impossible*, where the special agent had a choice of whether they wanted to accept the mission.

Jonah doesn't say much about Nineveh's wickedness, but the prophet Nahum gives us more insight. Nahum says that Nineveh was guilty of (1) evil plots against God (Nahum 1:9); (2) exploitation of the helpless (Nahum 2:12); (3) cruelty in war (Nahum 2:12-13); and (4) idolatry, prostitution, and witchcraft (Nahum 3:4).

God told Jonah to go to Nineveh, about 500 miles northeast of Israel, to warn of judgment and to declare that the people could receive God's mercy and forgiveness if they repented.

Review of Level 1

A. God gives the instructions.
B. God gives direction.
C. God gives location.

³ But *Jonah ran away* to Tarshish <u>to escape from the presence of the LORD</u> [and *his duty as His prophet*]. He *went down* to Joppa and found a ship going to Tarshish [*the most remote of the Phoenician trading cities*]. So he paid the fare and *went down* into the ship to go with them to Tarshish <u>away from the presence of the LORD.</u>

We see in verse 3 that Jonah had a negative response to God's command and fled from the presence of God. People flee God's presence when they don't want to hear what He has to say. This is a relationship lesson for everyone. Have you noticed in your life that people often leave your presence when they don't want to hear you? In God's presence, we will hear God's voice.

Now, it's easy for us to look at someone else's situation and judge and make opinions like we don't fail God also. Jonah had a real issue with the people of Nineveh and wanted them to be judged and punished.

How many of us have issues with people and have wished that

God would just do something bad to them?

Jonah knew God had a specific job for him, but he didn't want to do it. Tarshish was one of Phoenicia's western ports; Nineveh was to the northeast. Jonah was trying to get as far away from God's assignment as possible. We often go the opposite way when God gives us directions through His word. We run in fear, stubbornness, and perhaps even claim that God is asking too much. It may have been fear, but it was more likely anger at the generosity of God's mercy that made Jonah run. But running from God got him into worse trouble. Disobedience always leads you away from God. In the end, Jonah accepted that doing what God asks in the first place is far better. But by then, he had paid a costly price for running.

Disobedience is always costly. Sin will take you farther than you want to go, keep you longer than you want to stay, and cost you more than you want to pay.

⁴ But the LORD hurled a great wind toward the sea, and there was a violent tempest on the sea so that the ship was about to break up.

It's amazing that Jonah would try to run from the God of all things. Jonah underestimated God and must have forgotten that God controls the wind, water, waves, and whales.

⁵ Then the sailors were afraid, and each man cried out to his god; and to lighten the ship [and diminish the danger] they threw the ship's cargo into the sea. But Jonah had <u>gone below</u> into the hold of the ship and had lain down and was sound asleep.

While the storm raged, Jonah was sound asleep below deck. Even as he ran from God, Jonah's actions apparently didn't bother his conscience. But the absence of guilt isn't always a barometer of whether we are doing what is right. Because we can shut out God and deny reality, we cannot measure obedience by our feelings. Instead, we must compare what we do with God's standards of living.

Jonah's disobedience to God endangered the lives of the ship's crew. We have a great responsibility to obey God's word. Our sins and disobedience affect us and can hurt others around us. Isn't it amazing that in trouble, people cry out to who they consider God? This verse shows us that there is a difference between a god and God. And this story allows our God to show Himself mighty. Disobedience will always take you down.

Level 2 - A Person

⁶ <u>So the captain came up to him</u> and said, "How can you stay asleep? Get up! Call on your god! Perhaps your god will give a thought to us so that we will not perish."

The captain was the first person to address Jonah about his sleeping and confronted him about it. God had stepped up his level of communication to make it clear to Jonah that he was talking to him through another voice that was tangible. God had already spoken to him personally, and the captain was the level 2 person trying to make the connection.

⁷ And they said to another, "Come, let us cast lots, so we may learn who is to blame for this disaster." <u>So they cast lots and the lot fell on Jonah.</u>

The crew cast lots to find the guilty person, relying on their superstition to give them the answer. They believed that the gods spoke through the dice. Though Jonah ran, it didn't stop the dice from falling against him. Their system worked, but only because God used it to intervene, letting Jonah know that he couldn't run away.

Proverbs 16:33 New Living Translation (NLT)

³³ We may throw the dice, but the LORD determines how they fall.

Back into Jonah.

⁸ Then they said to him, "Now tell us! Who is to blame for this disaster? What is your occupation? Where do you come from? What is your country?" ⁹ So he said to them, "<u>I am a Hebrew, and I [reverently] fear and worship the LORD, the God of</u>

heaven, who made the sea and the dry land."

The interrogation begins.

- A. What is your occupation? Prophet/mouthpiece for God.
- B. Where did you come from? The Hebrew nation.
- C. What is your country? Israel.

Jonah made it clear that he knew his call and who he served. And yet, he ran from the God that controls the sea. It's amazing to me how we sometimes believe that we can run from the plans of God without being dealt with. Let me help you. God will have you do things you don't want to do in His name. God will have you deal with situations you don't want to deal with in His name. God will get you out of your comfort zone in His name. We need to stop looking for comfort and convenience in our service to the Lord.

10 Then the men became extremely frightened and said to him, "How could you do this?" For the men knew that he was running from the presence of the LORD, because he had told them.

If this is not a slap in the face, the sailors asked him the question, "How could you do this?" Another way of saying it is, "What were you thinking?" "Are you crazy?" "you must have lost your mind?"

Level 3 – Problems - The Winds and Waves against them

¹¹ Then they said to him, "What should we do to you, so that the sea will become calm for us?"—for the <u>sea was becoming more and more violent.</u> ¹² Jonah said to them, "<u>Pick me up and throw me into the sea.</u> Then the sea will become calm for you, <u>for I know that it is because of me that this great storm has come upon you.</u>"

You cannot seek God's help and run from Him at the same time. Jonah soon realized that no matter where he went, he couldn't escape God. But before Jonah could return to God, he first had to stop going in the opposite direction.

What has God told you to do that you have not done?

If you want more of God's assistance, you must be willing to carry out the assignments and responsibilities He gives you. You cannot say that you truly believe in God if you don't do what He says (1 John 2:3-6).

Jonah knew that he had disobeyed God and that the storm was his fault, but he didn't say anything until the crew cast lots and the lot fell on him (1:7). Then Jonah decided he would rather die to save the sailors than do anything to save the people of Nineveh. Jonah's hatred for the Assyrians and resentment toward God for loving them had poisoned his perspective.

"You have to be careful who you fellowship with and which fellows you allow in your ship because their problems can easily become your problems."

¹³ *Nevertheless, the men rowed hard [breaking through the waves] to return to land, but they could not, because the sea became even more violent [surging higher] against them.*

By trying to save Jonah's life, the sailors showed more compassion than Jonah, who did not want to warn the Ninevites of the coming judgment of God. Believers should be embarrassed when unbelievers show more concern and compassion than they do. God wants us to be concerned for all His people, lost and saved. Jonah gave them the solution to their problem, but the men still tried to row home. Don't forget that God controls the winds, the water, and the whale. God gave them a problem that only Jonah, being thrown overboard, could fix.

¹⁴ *Then they called on the LORD and said, "Please, O LORD, do not let us perish because of taking this man's life, and do not make us accountable for innocent blood; for You, O LORD, have done as You pleased."*

Notice when trials come, people have no problem calling on

God. Our relationship with God should not only be 911 calls but a daily dialogue for every situation and circumstance.

15 So they picked up Jonah and threw him into the sea, and the sea stopped its raging.

The problem is solved when obedience to the prophet's word is obeyed. Jonah was still a prophet and knew what needed to be done. At this point, Jonah was willing to sacrifice his life for the sailors but not the people of Nineveh. My brothers and sisters, hear me and hear me well. There are some people in your life that you must throw overboard to make it to your destination. And once you do, you will see your life calm down. Peace will come when some people leave.

16 Then the men greatly feared the LORD, and they offered a sacrifice to the LORD and <u>made vows</u>.

They were in awe of God when they saw the result of throwing Jonah overboard. As a result, the ship's crew began to worship God. It's amazing how people come to their senses after God moves and quickly forget and go back to their old ways. When God moves in your life, it's a great time to rededicate yourself to Him.

17 Now the LORD had <u>prepared (appointed, destined) a great fish to swallow Jonah.</u> And Jonah was in the stomach of the fish <u>three days and three nights.</u>

I love how God supplies a solution to Jonah's problem to get him back on course. We see the words prepared, appointed, and destined. God had a plan and purpose that would not be thwarted by Jonah's disobedience. While Jonah disobeyed, God was creating a solution. God is not surprised and is always ready with a solution. We can't outrun God, for He has a way of getting us back on track.

Remember, disobedience leads to discomfort.

Level 4 - Pain

Jonah 2 (AMP)

Jonah's Prayer

[1] Then <u>Jonah prayed to the Lord</u> his God from the stomach of the fish, [2] and said, "<u>I called out of my trouble and distress</u> to the Lord, and He answered me; out of the belly of Sheol I cried for help, <u>and You heard my voice</u>.

Amid his suffering, Jonah cried out to God in prayer. Prayer is our connection to infinite wisdom, and through prayer, we build our relationship with God. And Jonah was in dire need of some repairs to that relationship. We see in the verses below that when people are going through tough times, it is wise to call on God.

Psalm 91:15 (NLT)

15 When they call on me, I will answer; I will be with them in trouble. I will rescue and honor them.

Psalm 50:15 (NLT)
15 Then call on me when you are in trouble, and I will rescue you, and you will give me glory."

We see here in Jonah 2:2 the words "trouble" and "distress." And the word "distress" means suffering from anxiety, sorrow, or pain. Jonah offered a prayer of thanksgiving and a cry for deliverance from the belly of the fish. God saved him from the raging sea, and Jonah was overwhelmed that he had escaped certain death. Even from inside the fish, Jonah's prayer was heard by God. We can pray anywhere and anytime, and God will always hear us. In the belly of the fish, Jonah was ready to submit to God's will and purpose for him. Jonah compared his predicament in the belly of the fish to being in the land of the dead. His hard heart had been humbled by God's mercy toward him.

This verse lets us know that when we confess our sins, God can restore us.

James 5:16 (AMP)
16 Therefore, <u>confess your sins to one another [your false steps, your offenses], and pray for one another, that you may be healed and restored.</u> The heartfelt and persistent prayer of a

righteous man (believer) can accomplish much [when put into action and made effective by God—it is dynamic and can have tremendous power].

Jonah lets us know that God remembers us despite our failures. **Jonah 2:7** should give us peace.

> *Jonah 2:7 "When my soul was fainting within me, <u>I remembered the Lord, And my prayer came to You, Into Your holy temple</u>.*

Jonah said, "As my life was slipping away, I remembered the LORD." Often, we act the same way. When life is going well, we tend to take God for granted, but when we lose hope, we cry out to Him. This kind of relationship with God can result only in an inconsistent, up-and-down spiritual life. A consistent, daily commitment to God promotes a solid relationship with Him.

Questions

1. How does God want to speak to us?

2. If we don't listen to our mentors, who will God use to speak to us?

3. What was Jonah's job?

4. Why did Jonah run from God?

5. Have you ever run from an assignment that God gave you?

6. Who was the first person to confront Jonah?

7. What was the problem that God presented Jonah with?

8. What is the pain that Jonah had to deal with?

9. What was God's solution to Jonah's running?

10. What was God's plan for saving Jonah?

11. Has God ever used a person to speak to you after He tried to talk to you personally? How did it make you feel?

12. Can you remember a problem that you had that stemmed from you not listening to God?

13. Have you ever had to pray and ask God to forgive you for your disobedience?

14. What were the consequences of that action?

15. Have you ever allowed your negative feelings for someone to cloud your judgement?

16. What made Jonah change his tune?

17. How did God respond to Jonah's prayer?

Chapter Three

God's Voice Sounds Like Your Spiritual Authority

We have established that God wants to have a relationship with us and speak to us personally. So, the next logical question is, what does God sound like?

All of us have had distinctive voices in our lives that are instantly recognizable. I know that my mother would say my name and I would know how she felt about me by how she said my name. The voices could have been a mother or father, a grandmother, a coach, or a military superior, but the bottom line is you would not have to see them to recognize who was talking. We need to grow to a place with God that His voice is distinct.

The Bible lets us know in **Genesis 1:26** that we are made in God's image and God's likeness. So, if we have a distinct voice, God has a distinct voice. And much like a baby recognizes their parents' voice, we should do the same with God.

Genesis 1:26-28 (AMP)
26 Then God said, "Let Us (Father, Son, Holy Spirit) make man in Our image, according to Our likeness [not physical, but a spiritual personality and moral likeness]; and let them have complete authority over the fish of the sea, the birds of the air, the cattle, and over the entire earth, and over

everything that creeps and crawls on the earth." ²⁷ So God created man in His own image, in the image and likeness of God He created him; male and female He created them.

And we know from Genesis that God spoke to Adam and Eve (Genesis 2-3). So, it's a natural question to ask what God sounds like. In this passage of **1 Samuel 3**, we will get some clues on how God sounds. We also learn that God doesn't just call you once; He will repeatedly try to get your attention. In the passage, we see that God is trying to get to a young prophet named Samuel through his teacher, Eli. Let's jump into the text.

1 Samuel 3 (AMP)

¹ Now the boy Samuel was attending to the service of the Lord under the supervision of Eli. <u>The word of the Lord was rare and precious in those days; visions [that is, new revelations of divine truth] were not widespread.</u>

The second part of this verse is where the revelation is for me. It speaks of the word of the Lord being rare in those days. It also implies the purpose of Samuel, for Samuel was going to be the answer to the word being rare. God was going to use Samuel to be His mouthpiece. Samuel was going to be the prophet that God wanted. Samuel was a gift from his mother, Hannah, to God. She told the Lord that if He gave her a child, she would give it back, and his hair would never be cut. So, she dedicated Samuel to the Lord. (1 Samuel 1-2)

Now we're going to see the introduction of God's voice to Samuel.

² Yet it happened at that time, as Eli was lying down in his own place (now his eyesight had begun to grow dim and he could not see well). ³ and the [oil] lamp of God had not yet gone out, and Samuel was lying down in the temple of the Lord, where the ark of God was, ⁴ <u>that the Lord called Samuel, and he answered, "Here I am." ⁵ He ran to Eli and said, "Here I am, for you called me." But Eli said, "I did not call you; lie down again."</u> So he went and lay down.

Here, we see God makes a direct appeal to Samuel, but Samuel runs to Eli. Eli is his teacher, mentor, and father figure. This verse gives us insight that God will often sound like your teacher. Remember, God wants to speak to us personally first.

Samuel did not know the voice of God and had to learn God's voice for himself. This is a great teaching point for all of us. We must learn how God speaks to us. So we're not hostage to anyone else's interpretation of what God wants to tell us.

⁶ <u>Then the Lord called yet again, "Samuel!" So Samuel got up and went to Eli and said, "Here I am, for you called me."</u> But Eli answered, "I did not call, my son; lie down again." ⁷ <u>Now Samuel did not yet know [or personally experience] the Lord, and the word of the Lord was not yet revealed [directly] to him. ⁸ So the Lord called Samuel a third time</u>. And he stood and *went to Eli and said, "Here I am, for you did call me." Then Eli understood that it was the Lord [who was] calling the boy.*

We see here that God is persistent in trying to speak to Samuel and keeps on calling him until he answers.

Question: Have you answered God yet?

⁹ So Eli said to Samuel, "Go, lie down, and it shall be that if He calls you, you shall say, 'Speak, Lord, for Your servant is listening.'" So Samuel went and lay down in his place.

Now, we see the next level of communication: God is now letting Eli inform Samuel that He wants to talk. Remember, we learned in the last chapter that God wants to speak to us personally, and if that fails, He will use a person.

Eli then gives him instructions on what to do when God calls him. He says, "The next time God calls your name, say this: 'Speak Lord, your servant is listening.'"

My friends, you need to make this a part of your faith walk. "Lord, speak. Your servant is listening." I do this all the time when I'm alone with God.

¹⁰ Then the Lord came and stood and called as at the previous times, "Samuel! Samuel!" Then Samuel answered, "Speak, for Your servant is listening."

We see here that Samuel follows instructions perfectly. Obedience is the catalyst to breakthrough. If you want to hear from God consistently, you must be a good listener. Samuel took Eli at his word, and we must take God at His word.

¹¹ The Lord said to Samuel, "Behold, I am about to do a thing in Israel at which both ears of everyone who hears it will ring. ¹² On that day <u>I will carry out against Eli everything that I have spoken concerning his house (family), from beginning to end.</u> ¹³ Now <u>I have told him that I am about to judge his house forever for the sinful behavior which he knew [was happening], because his sons were bringing a curse on themselves [dishonoring and blaspheming God] and he did not rebuke them.</u> ¹⁴ Therefore I have sworn to the house of Eli that the sinful behavior of Eli's house (family) shall not be atoned for by sacrifice or offering forever."

God speaks to Samuel and gives him the word for the time, but the challenge was it was not something that Samuel wanted to hear or to deliver. God tells Samuel that his father figure, his mentor, is about to be judged harshly. It's amazing in this passage that we see that God lets Samuel know He tried to speak to Eli personally, but he didn't listen. So now you're going to tell him what I told him about his sons. They are about to be judged for what they have done. There it is again; God tries to speak personally and then through people.

15 So Samuel lay down until morning. Then he opened the doors of the Lord's house. But Samuel was afraid to tell the vision to Eli. 16 But Eli called Samuel and said, "Samuel, my son." And he answered, "Here I am." 17 Then Eli said, "What is it that He said to you? Please do not hide it from me. May God do the same to you, and more also, if you hide from me anything of all that He said to you." 18 So Samuel told him everything, hiding nothing from him. And Eli said, "It is the Lord; may He do what seems good to Him."

The next day, Samuel wakes up, and he's confronted by his mentor, Eli, and is asked to give an account of what God had to say. I know this had to be a difficult conversation, having to deliver the message of judgment to the person he honored so much.

Eli said, "It is the Lord. May He do what seems good to Him." Some may wonder why Eli responded so positively. Well, because God had been trying to tell him the message that Samuel had told him. So, it was unsurprising to him when he was echoing what God had already told him. Remember, God always wants to talk to us personally before he sends a person. The struggle with hearing God's voice, for Eli, was he loved his sons more than he loved obeying God. He allowed his children to sin against God, and now they were going to suffer the consequences of disobedience.

19 Now Samuel grew; and the Lord was with him and He let none of his words [c]fail [to be fulfilled]. 20 And all Israel from Dan [in the north] to Beersheba [in the south] knew that Samuel was appointed as a prophet of the Lord. 21 And the Lord continued to appear in Shiloh, for the Lord revealed Himself to Samuel in Shiloh by the word of the Lord.

In this amazing passage, we see that none of the words of Samuel failed. This basically lets us know that whatever Samuel said happened. I believe this was the case because Samuel was constantly communicating with God, and God used Samuel as His mouthpiece to the people.

In verse 21, we see the Lord reveal Himself to Samuel by the word of God. The word of God is the voice of God in print.

In the verses below, you will see the four P's by which God tried to communicate to Eli.

Review

Level 1 - God speaks to Eli Personally - 1 Samuel 2:12-36

Level 2 - God speaks through a Person; Samuel - 1 Samuel 3

Level 3 - God speaks through Problems: 1 Samuel 4:12-18 - The death of his children

Level 4 - God speaks through Pain; Eli broke his neck and died - 1 Samuel 4:18

1 Kings 19 gives us some more clues to how God sounds.

Let's jump into the passage.

1 Kings 19 (NLT)
¹ When Ahab got home, he told Jezebel everything Elijah had done, including the way he had killed all the prophets of Baal. ² So Jezebel sent this message to Elijah: "May the gods strike me and even kill me if by this time tomorrow I have not killed you just as you killed them." ³ Elijah was afraid and fled for his life. He went to Beersheba, a town in Judah, and he left his servant there. ⁴ Then he went on alone into the wilderness, traveling all day. He sat down under a solitary broom tree and prayed that he might die. "I have had enough, Lord," he said. "Take my life, for I am no better than my ancestors who have already died."

Elijah had just had a great victory over the prophets of Baal in the prior chapter. And you would think he would be on cloud nine, but that was not the case. A powerful woman named Jezebel threatened to kill him, and he fled for his life. It's amazing how he was bold as a lion in one moment, and in the next moment, he was fearfully running for his life.

You notice it says that he left his servant behind, and he was alone. One of the key aspects of God speaking to us is us being alone. Elijah was so frustrated with the situation he asked God to kill him. I don't know if you've ever been so frustrated that you just wanted God to take your life. This story should give us some solace that even though Elijah was a mighty man of God, he still had his moments of weakness. Thank God we could serve a God who uses broken vessels.

⁵ Then he lay down and slept under the broom tree. But as he was sleeping, an angel touched him and told him, "Get up and eat!" ⁶ He looked around and there beside his head was some bread baked on hot stones and a jar of water! So he ate and drank and lay down again. ⁷ Then the angel of the Lord came again and touched him and said, "Get up and eat some more, or the journey ahead will be too much for you." ⁸ So he got up and ate and drank, and the food gave him enough strength to travel forty days and forty nights to Mount Sinai, the mountain of God. ⁹ There he came to a cave, where he spent the night.

Elijah isolated himself and put himself in a place where he could hear God. You'll notice the prescription that God gave him through an angel was rest and food. So, when you see someone fearful, anxious, worried, or stressed, the prescription might be rest and food. I love how the angel said the journey ahead was too much for him without food. This should excite us by knowing that God knew where Elijah was going to be. That should give you peace that God is the author and the finisher of your faith. So whatever you're going through, God is in your tomorrow today. After 40 days of travel, Elijah showed up for his appointment to have a conversation with God. Now we're going to see God start the conversation, and we will get some insight into what God sounds like.

But the Lord said to him, "<u>What are you doing here, Elijah?</u>" [10] *Elijah replied, "I have zealously served the Lord God Almighty. But the people of Israel have broken their covenant with you, torn down your altars, and killed every one of your prophets. I am the only one left, and now they are trying to kill me, too."*

Elijah tells God about his struggle as if God does not already know his struggle, and he lets God know but that he is the only one standing up for God. Now God gives him the prerequisite to hearing the voice.

[11] *"Go out and stand before me on the mountain," the Lord told him. And as Elijah stood there, the Lord passed by, and a mighty windstorm hit the mountain. It was such a terrible blast that the rocks were torn loose, but the Lord was not in the wind. After the wind there was an earthquake, but the Lord was not in the earthquake.* [12] *And after the earthquake there was a fire, but the Lord was not in the fire. And after the fire there was the sound of <u>a gentle whisper</u>.*

We see here some distinguishing characteristics of God's voice. It was not mighty like a windstorm. It was not terrible that it would blast the rocks. It was not rattling like an earthquake. It was not roaring like a fire but a gentle whisper. Now, this will help us to better position ourselves to hear Him. For us to hear a gentle whisper, we must be silent and learn how to practice silence. Most understand the part of us talking to God, but few understand our responsibility in listening to God.

[13] *When Elijah heard it, he wrapped his face in his cloak and went out and stood at the entrance of the cave. And a voice said, "What are you doing here, Elijah?"*

Again, we see God asking him, "What are you doing here?"
Why are you off track?
Why have you lost focus?
Why have you taken your eye off the ball?

You will notice that in the verse, it was fear that got Elijah out of position.

[14] *He replied again, "I have zealously served the Lord God Almighty. But the people of Israel have broken their covenant with you, torn down your altars, and killed every one of your prophets. I am the only one left, and now they are trying to kill me, too."*

Have you ever noticed that people repeat themselves when they are out of position? And they have many excuses? As you heard in the last passage Elijah repeats himself in explaining to God why he's out of position.

15 Then the Lord told him, "Go back the same way you came, and travel to the wilderness of Damascus. When you arrive there, anoint Hazael to be king of Aram. 16 Then anoint Jehu grandson of Nimshi to be king of Israel, and anoint Elisha son of Shaphat from the town of Abel-meholah to replace you as my prophet. 17 Anyone who escapes from Hazael will be killed by Jehu, and those who escape Jehu will be killed by Elisha! 18 Yet I will preserve 7,000 others in Israel who have never bowed down to Baal or kissed him!"

Much like the story of our friend, Jonah, God did not change His assignment even though he lost his way. What God has called for you is for you, and you may run from the mission, but God is still going to ask you to fulfill it. God tells Elijah to return to where he came from and finish his assignment. God gives him instructions on who he was supposed to anoint and position for the next season. And then, in His closing argument, God tells him that he is not the only one taking a stand for Him. *"I have seven thousand men in the city right now who will not bow down to Baal."* God made sure that Elijah knew he was not alone in this journey.

The Five Characteristics of God's Voice

1. **God's Voice is Peaceful** - Col. 3:15 - Peace of God: It rules by peace, not tension and stress, internal calmness, and has nothing to do with external things around you.

2. **God's Voice is Not Fear Based** - 2 Tim. 1:7 - God doesn't use fear as a tool.

3. **God's voice is Not High Pressure** - Isaiah 28:16, 52:12 - God's voice will not rush you, with quick deadlines. God is not governed by time. You are going to make mistakes moving too quickly.

4. **God's voice speaks Good Things** - Phil. 4:8, 2 Chronicles 7:14, Is. 1:18 - God speaks good things. The gospel is the good news. God will give it to you in a positive way.

5. **God's voice will be in harmony with His Word** - 2 Tim. 3:15-17 - It will always be in harmony with the word of God, it won't violate scriptures.

Questions

1. Whose voice do you know without seeing them?

2. Have you ever felt like God was speaking to you through someone else?

3. When God is calling you, what should your response be?

4. What were God's instructions to Samuel?

5. Why do you think God spoke to Samuel instead of Eli?

6. How did Eli respond to Samuel's message?

7. Do you sometimes struggle with telling someone the truth that might hurt them?

8. How do you overcome the fear and be real with them?

9. What was Elijah fearful of?

10. What was God's prescription for Elijah's problem?

11. What did God tell Elijah to do?

12. Has God ever told you to finish what you started?

13. Have you ever felt like you were the only one serving?

Chapter Four

Tuned In

Every now and then, we must take our cars in for a tune-up. A tune-up is needed to ensure everything is in working order and functioning to its highest capabilities. Without tune-ups, our cars will have unnecessary breakdowns. And just like a car needs a tune-up, our ears need to be tuned in to the voice of God.

Proverbs 2:1 says, "***My child listen to what I say***, *treasure my commands...*"

We must be mindful that when we are not in tune, we will find ourselves in places we should not be. We must consistently tune in to hear His voice because He's always talking. I think that's why Jesus said ***my sheep hear my voice, a stranger they will not follow (John 10:27)***. The verse also helps us understand that there are other voices that are creating noise that can deter us and distract us from His voice.

If we are not tuned in, we miss out! We miss out on where God intended us to be, which is inevitably the best place for us.

There is a frequency by which God speaks, and it's always flowing, but it takes time, patience, and stillness for us to tap into the frequency. The Bible says that ***you will hear me in a still small voice* (1 Kings 19:12)**. To be clear, I do not have a formula for hearing God. I've just heard Him in certain spaces and times when I was still, quiet, and patiently waiting.

Our hunger for God's Word is a precursor to being able to tune into God's frequency. The Bible says that *the righteous hunger and thirst for Him (Matthew 5:6)*. When we think of the woman with the issue of blood crawling and pressing her way through was hungry **(Luke 8)**. Zacchaeus, racing ahead of the crowd and sitting in the tree to see Jesus, was hungry **(Luke 19)**. The blind leper cried out, "Jesus, have mercy on me!" —he was hungry **(Mark 10)**. What were they hungry for? They were hungering for more of God. In the process of searching for God, they got more of everything else they needed.

Proverbs 2:2 *"Tune your ears to wisdom, concentrate on understanding."*

Some of you know of this beloved thing, the "Cable/Internet Router."

When storms come in, and you can't watch your TV show, you call your cable provider for assistance.

Question: When you go home and you can't tune into what you want to tune into, how long does it take for you to call your service provider for help?

How long?

I remember when the Floyd Mayweather fight was coming on, and I couldn't get reception. I called our provider and said, **"Hey man, I paid a hundred dollars, and I can't see the fight!"** It's amazing the lengths we will go to get what we value doing. I realize that at times, we will rush home to watch our favorite show and change our schedule to watch our favorite game, and if you come home and your router doesn't work, it will be a misunderstanding.

Question: When was the last time you tuned in to God with total focus and no distractions?

What I realize is that when we can't tune in to our program, we call someone for help. It seems like we usually tune in to God when we're stuck in a rut. When our money is funny and our change is strange, it seems like our ears perk up.

It's like it has to be an emergency for us to listen.

- When the person you love leaves
- When the doctor reports come back with a negative report
- When the check bounces
- Why?

We call the cable company because we understand that they have a solution to our problem to get us reconnected. And too often in our walk with God, we don't reach out to God when our connection is broken. Being lost is often an indicator that you have lost connection with God. Like many of us who have gotten poor directions, we end up in places we did not intend to be. I know we have gotten lost and gone astray at some point in our lives. The real question is, who will you call for help and guidance? I hope it's not the ghostbusters.

All of us, like sheep, have strayed away. We have left God's paths to follow our own. Yet the Lord laid on him the sins of us all. Isaiah 53:6 (NLT)

Question: When was the last time you tuned in to God? The Bible says, *"Tune in your ears to wisdom and concentrate..."* meaning to tune in, you're going to have to tune some stuff out.

And we wonder why we can't hear God but spend all our time listening to junk. I don't know what your unproductive habit may be, but we all could do better in our choices of time spent with God versus other things. If you want to help yourself, let's do a simple exercise. I want you to track what you do for a couple of days and categorize those activities into two sections: Productive and Unproductive.

I love technology, but there are some definite downsides. I hate those earbuds that go in your ears so you can hear through Bluetooth. I hate them because you can't see them and assume people are listening to or talking to you, but they are in another world. Have you ever tried to call your child? And they are bobbing their heads or laughing but cannot hear you? Oh, Jesus, I hate it. Then I have to raise my voice to be heard. Family, there are so many devices fighting to get in our ears.

Question: How many times has God tried to talk to you, and you do this?

These are some examples of things that we tend to say when we're not in tune with God's voice:

- *"No, I'm good, God..."*
- *"Let me finish my song, please."*
- *What...wait, wait, wait, God.*

And God is saying, "I got to talk to you right now."

When God is trying to tune you in, are you ready to listen?

If you're not careful, you will allow the wrong things to get in your ear. We must tune out things that are not feeding our faith and tune out doubt, fear, and unbelief. We miss signals when we are not paying attention to the signal caller.

Proverbs 2:3 _**Cry out for insight**_ _and_ _**ask**_ _for understanding._

Often, when God is trying to talk to you, He seems to catch you by yourself. Situations and circumstances are going to hit your life, and you're going to be saying, _**"Lord, I don't know what to do. I've done everything I can in my own strength. What am I supposed to do?"**_

Cry out because you don't have a way. Cry out because you don't have an answer. Cry out!

Let's look at Matthew 7
Matthew 7:7. Look at what it says: _**Ask and keep on asking and it shall be given to you; seek and keep on seeking and you will find; knock and keep on knocking and**_ _**the door be opened.**_

Question: Have you kept on? The act of persistently asking God is an indicator of your faith that He can do it. How many situations have you stopped asking God about? Don't stop. Keep asking, keep seeking, keep knocking, and don't quit on it. We serve a God that can do exceedingly and abundantly. Keep asking, don't quit, don't quit, don't quit. God promises to answer us as Jer. 33:3 tells us.

Jeremiah 33:3 (AMP)

3 'Call to Me and I will answer you, and tell you [and even show you] great and mighty things, [things which have been confined and hidden], which you do not know and understand and cannot distinguish.

The enemy is not after you; he's after what your faith can produce. That's why the Bible says *if you have the faith of a mustard seed you will speak to your mountains (Matthew 17:20).* Your mountain-moving power is in your faith, and you must keep your faith in check. You have to speak to your mountains because if you're not careful, your mountains will start to talk to you. And you can allow the voice of your mountain(obstacle) to speak louder than the Word. Keep asking, keep seeking, keep knocking, for everyone who keeps on asking receives, who keeps on seeking finds, and he who keeps on knocking, the door will be opened to them.

We must fight as **2 Timothy 4:7** tell us.

2 Timothy 4:7: *Fight the good fight, finish the course, keep the faith.*

We must search like **Proverbs 2:4:** *"Search for them as you would for silver and seek them as hidden treasure."*

We must seek like **Matthew 6:33** says *Seek ye...first and most importantly, aim, strive after His kingdom and His* *righteousness. His way of doing and being right, the attitude and the character of God, and all these things.*

You must make up your mind that I am a seeker; I need more of God; I need more revelation; I need help, Father. I can't do it without you."

I'm seeking Him; I'm thirsting for Him; I need more of God. As the Bible says, as you seek Him first, all else shall be added unto you.

Proverbs 2:5 says *Then you will understand what it means to fear the Lord and you will gain knowledge.*

The beginning of knowledge is the fear of God. Not fear as if you're scared of God, but understanding, reverential fear, understanding that God sees all and God knows all and God's plan for your life is better than your plan.

Proverbs 9:10 (NLT) says *The fear of the Lord is the foundation of wisdom. Knowledge of the Holy One results in good judgment.*

So, the beginning of wisdom is understanding God and knowing His ways, for His ways are perfect. I don't know about you, but I used to be one of those who like to put things together without instructions. I would look at the picture on the box and believe, with my inherent gift of knowledge, that I could put it together without the instructions. Does anybody know what I'm talking about? So, I decided that when we bought my son a basketball hoop, I would assemble it without instructions. I said to myself, *"This is not deep. It's a pole, a weight at the bottom, and you put the rim there."* So, I went ahead, and I'm doing what I do, and the last piece is supposed to go on, and I realize I have the rim on backwards. I then take it all apart and do it all over again with the help of instructions. Have you ever tried to do things in your own strength? I have now concluded that,

"Stupid, the instructions were made by the owner, and the owner knows how to put it together. So, therefore, it is wise to listen to the instructions..."

So why do we think we will win this thing called life by doing it with our own instructions? If God left some instructions for us to have a good life, wouldn't it make sense that we read the instructions? Following instructions are essential to our journey with God.

So now, in the new dispensation of Jomo, I get instructions, look at all the parts, and count them; one, two, three, four. I lay it out and go slow, and now my wife says, *"You're so handy now! You never used to be handy."* We would always have to pay somebody to fix stuff that I just never finished. But now, I understand that the beginning of knowledge is knowing Him, and since He is all-knowing and I am a child of His, I have the same access to knowledge that He does. So now I sit back and say, *"Lord, I need your wisdom for this?"*

Family, we must get this. When we acquire knowledge, we will get revelation. And when we get revelation, we get direction. So, we have to get this knowledge, and if we get knowledge, we will get the revelation. If we get revelation, we get understanding. If we get understanding, we get direction.

Proverbs 2:5: *Then you will understand what it means to fear the Lord and you will gain knowledge. For the Lord grants wisdom.*

The Lord grants wisdom. From the mouth come knowledge and understanding. Now, God can grant wisdom, but there's also a way you can get wisdom through thirsting and hungering for wisdom. God will give you more. That's what **James 1:5** says *if anyone lacks the wisdom to ask God.* And He will give it to you liberally.

Proverbs 2:7, I like this one: He grants a treasure. *He grants a treasure of common sense to the honest. He is a shield to those who walk with integrity.*

Common sense sure isn't common. Come on, you all know that! Have you ever thought to yourself?

"Don't you have common sense?

Why did you go do that?

That doesn't make any sense."

Proverbs 2:8 *He guards the paths of the just and protects those who are faithful to him.*

The key point is you will find the right way to go, and now, you'll hear His voice.

Now, these are the prerequisites, the requirements to hear His voice, and if you get this, it will change your life. The beginning is understanding that your way does not work and you must get sick and tired of being sick and tired of yourself. You must be tired of being stuck. You must be sick of asking these questions:

- *"Why am I always here?*
- *Why does it seem to always happen to me?*
- *I know I should be better than I'm doing, yet I'm here again."*

No doubt that was me, and I had a conversation with myself. I said, ***"Dude come on, man, you're making a mess of yourself. I know you're better than what you're doing, but what's up with this?"*** And I talked to myself, and I wrote some new rules. Everyone needs to ask themselves, ***"What are my new rules for my life?"***

In your life, if we don't learn from our mistakes, we're doomed to repeat them. So, I've learned that every time I made a mess of myself, I did an autopsy. I exhumed the body and learned from my mistakes.

Proverbs 2:9-10 *⁹ Then you will understand what is right, just, and fair, and you will find the right way to go. ¹⁰ For wisdom will enter your heart, and knowledge will fill you with joy.*

Four things I want you to hear in verses 9 and 10

Number One - We must trust and honor God.

Number Two - We must realize the Bible reveals God's wisdom for us. It's the blueprint for our life.

Number Three - We must make a lifelong series of right choices. Come on, "*choices.*" Your life is based on the choices and decisions and the consequences that come with them.

Number Four - Learn from your mistakes. The Bible says *only a fool returns to his vomit (Proverbs 26:11),* meaning where you made a mess of yourself, why would you return to that spot? And often, we do, just to see if there would be no repercussions.

Wisdom Keys

Number One: Jesus and the Word are one

John 1:1 says, *"In the beginning was the Word, the Word was with God, the Word was God."*

Revelation 19:13 (AMP) *[13] He is dressed in a robe dipped in blood, and His name is called The Word of God.*

The Word and Jesus are one and the same. And the more Word I know, the more about Jesus I know. The more of God's Word I allow in my mind, the more my mind is being transformed into the mind of Christ. As I go through the transformation of thinking like Christ, I will begin to walk like Christ. The Bible says in Phil. 2:5 *"Let this mind be in you that was also in Christ Jesus."* So, as I get more Word in me, I get more of Christ's mind in me. One of the key aspects of a successful life is what you read and who you surround yourself with. Allow Jesus to be your building block.

And with the mind of Christ comes the understanding of the voice of God. So now, when I hear a word, I say that's Jesus. Why? The greater my understanding is for His word and His way grew, the greater my revelation became. And then people start to say, *"Man, you're smart."* Yes, I'm smart enough to know Jesus is the answer. You don't have to have all the answers, you just need to know who does, and *James 1:5 says, "If anyone lacks wisdom, ask God for He'll give it to you liberally."*

You will learn that if you can stay in this word frequently, you will start to develop the frequency of God.

The more of the Word you have, the more Jesus you have. Praise God.

Number Two: Study and Apply

Mark 4:24 (AMP)

²⁴ Then He said to them, "Pay attention to what you hear. By your own standard of measurement [that is, to the extent that you <u>study</u> spiritual truth and <u>apply</u> godly wisdom] it will be measured to you [and you will be given even greater ability to respond]—and more will be given to you besides.

The verse says **to the extent that you <u>study</u> spiritual truth and <u>apply</u> Godly wisdom, it will be measured to you and you will be given even greater ability... "**

Are you studying and applying?

Now how can you respond if you can't comprehend? He's saying the more Bible knowledge you get, the greater your ability to respond. It happens all the time in sports, the quarterback throws the ball this way, and the receiver goes the wrong way. Miscommunication happens every day in our world. God is sending signals. He throws alley-oops (a basketball terminology where the basketball is thrown in front of the rim for an assist), but we miss the signal because we're not tuned into Him. We need a tune-up! We need to call Jesus and say, **"Lord, fix my router! Lord, help me. I've gotten off the course. I've drifted too far. Help me, Lord!"**

You know, when you get too far out from the city, your cell phone will start to drop, and you can't make contact because you're too far away.

Look at what the verse says, **"...and more will be given to you."** If you can learn how to hear His voice, you will receive greater insight, and revelation comes.

God has good stuff for you, and people can't figure out how you got the promotion. People don't understand how you got that good deal. You got the deal because you could discern the voice. You received the promotion because you could hear the voice. You got the house because you could hear the voice.

Now, the question is, who determines your ability to hear His voice?

The answer is...you do.

We cannot be like Allen Iverson when he minimized the necessity of practice. We must practice being in His presence. Jesus replied in Luke 11:28, **"But even more blessed are all who hear the Word of God and put it into..."** what? **Practice!** I want you to practice being in His presence, just being still. If it was as simple as just getting in a room by yourself, fewer people would struggle with it. All right, so how do I practice being in His presence?

1. The key aspect of it is being still, and with being still, you must make sure you're in a place where you don't have distractions and other sounds going.

2. It's helpful if you can close your eyes because your eyes will lead you to other things. So I close my eyes and try to look through my spiritual eyes.

3. I often start with, "Lord, Is there something I need to know?"

4. Lord, show me what I need to see.

5. Lord, your servant is listening.

6. "Lord, I avail myself to you," and then I just sit still.

7. When you're trying to be still, it seems like every thought comes to mind. The email, the deadline, the call you're supposed to make, and the idea that you could not remember all seem to pop up when you're trying to be still. So, you must learn how to ignore those detours to hear His voice.

Lastly, hearing is based on relationships. Look what He says, **"Whoever is of God and belongs to Him hears the truth of God's Word, for this reason you do not hear them because you are not of God. (John 8:47)"** If you are not in fellowship with Him you can't hear Him, you better check yourself.

In June 2008, I was wrestling with what God told me to do. God said to start a church. I told my wife what God said. I was in the dining room on the floor praying, crying, and making a mess of myself at about 3:00 a.m. I told her what God told me to do, start a church, and she said, *"Get back down on your knees and ask God again."* What kind of encouragement is that? *"You better ask God again because He didn't tell me I'll be a pastor's wife, so you need to go and talk to Him one more time."* *"Babe..."* I said.

"Jomo," she said, *"go down to the county public schools and go ahead and do your paperwork to be a substitute teacher because if this church thing doesn't work out, you better figure out a way to make some money."*

This is my ID badge.

People say, *"Pastor, you don't look happy."* I was confused and struggling with what God told me to do. I was in the valley of decision, and God said, "Start a church." My wife wasn't quite sure because "Jomo" and "Pastor" didn't coincide, but she said, *"Jomo, do what God told you to do."*

I tell you this story, family, because some of you here today are in the valley of decision, and you have to make a decision. What did God tell you to do? There is a safe plan that comes with security. But God is telling you to go with Him in another direction.

See, there's a difference between God's will and your plan. God will let you stay in a place below His will for you if you choose. I'm so thankful I said yes to God years ago because I'd be a good substitute teacher. I would have gone back and gotten my certification and done all the stuff they told me to do, but that's not what God told me to do. Some of you right now are walking in the valley of decision, and you're trying to figure out what to do. I'm telling you today, hear His voice. His voice will be uncomfortable and take you out of your comfort zone. You'll feel like, ***"Lord, I don't know if it's going to work out."***

I gave up traveling as a high-paid speaker to start a church. If you don't know, people don't have to give to a church, and statistics state most don't give to a church. As a speaker, I knew I would be alright if I had a certain number of sales. The church is free will, meaning people do whatever they want to. They can come, they can go, they can leave. I like security; the church is not secure. All of us must make some choices. I keep this ID badge, and I look at it as my memory of the faith step, I had to take.

You're going to have to take a faith step to get what God has for you. You'll have to get out of the boat. I don't know what boat has you bound, but you've got to get up out of that boat. You've got to get out of your comfort zone. Comfort is not where God wants you. God wants you on the water. See, the miracles are on the water, but you don't know how it will work out. So, getting out of the boat starts with you tuning into God's voice. And for us to get the frequency of God, we must spend more time with God.

Remember: Frequently = Frequency

Questions

1. Have you ever had something break down on you because of your lack of maintenance?

2. If someone were to examine your life, what would they say you are tuned into?

3. Do you know what you need to tune out?

4. Do you consider yourself hungry for the things of God?

5. Do you think you tune into God enough?

6. Do you know how to connect with God?

7. Have you ever had an experience when you realized you had no control over the outcome?

8. Do you have a problem with taking instructions from those in authority?

9. Can you remember a time when not listening to instructions cost you dearly?

10. Have you settled for a life that is less than your potential?

Chapter Five

Spirit Led

One of the keys to hearing the voice of God is utilizing our internal antennas. God has given us the Holy Spirit to be our guide. In this chapter, we're going to learn about being Spirit-led listeners. Before we jump into this, I want you to get a proper context of the Holy Spirit. Once you have a relationship with Jesus, you have a relationship with the Holy Spirit; **John 14:16-17** confirms this.

16 And I will ask the Father, and he will give you another Advocate, who will never leave you. 17 He is the Holy Spirit, who leads into all truth. The world cannot receive him, because it isn't looking for him and doesn't recognize him. But you know him, because he lives with you now and later will be in you.

So to be clear, *"if you have Jesus, that means you have the Holy Spirit."*

Many people think the Holy Spirit's spooky or weird. For some reason, they understand God the father and Jesus the son, but the Holy Spirit gets no honor. And by having that thought process, we limit the Holy Spirit's ability in our lives. Where there is no honor, there is no respect, and where there is no respect, you cannot receive.

Now, let me break it down for you how we got here with the Holy Spirit. In the Garden of Eden, God spoke eye-to-eye with Adam and Eve, and it was not received. They rebelled against God by eating the fruit. So, God kicked them out of the garden. Then God said, "Let's go save mankind," so he sent Jesus to talk to mankind again eye-to-eye, and it was not received. The Bible says, **"They rejected the Chief Cornerstone (Mark 12:10)."** And now we have the Holy Spirit that was sent to assist us in receiving messages from God.

Key Point: Don't reject the Holy Spirit, just receive.

John Chapter 16 is the main text that we're going to be teaching from today. It says, **"I have many more things to say to you, but you cannot bear to hear them right now."**

Jesus couldn't tell them all that was to come because they were not ready to receive. They would not understand that He would be crucified and come back. It didn't make sense to them. *This verse lets us know that certain people cannot receive what we have. Ultimately, God will give you revelation on a level that's not on the level of others. So, when God gives you a vision, you may not find a co-signer because the vision was not for them. It was for you.*

Numbers 23:19 says, **"God is not a man that He shall lie nor the Son of man that He should repent."** I mention this because we have a hard time trusting God and just taking Him at His word.

John 16:13 (AMP) *13 But when He, the Spirit of Truth, comes, He will guide you into all the truth [full and complete truth]. For He will not speak on His own initiative, but He will speak whatever He hears [from the Father—the message regarding the Son], and He will disclose to you what is to come [in the future].*

He will guide you into all truth. Notice the capital truth and the lowercase truth. Here's a revelation: your facts will change, but the truth never does.

Fact: I had stage III colon cancer, but the truth was I was healed.

Fact: Your money may be funny, but the truth is you are wealthy.

Fact: You may feel unloved, but the truth is Christ died for you because you were loved.

The facts will change, but the truth remains the same. Make sure you put more confidence in the truth (the word of God) than your facts. Sometimes, your facts don't look good, but the truth doesn't change.

I was at the house, and our Wi-Fi was not working. We called Verizon, our service provider, and someone came to the house. Once there, they asked, "*Where is your main box?*" I told him that it was in the back room. He came out of the room in like 60 seconds and said, " *Everything is working. Somebody plugged out the connection."*

Key Point: We should always verify our connections with God.

Back into **John 16,** *"He will not speak on His own initiative, but He will speak whatever He hears from the father, the message regarding the Son, and He will disclose to you what is to come."* We often say, *"Something made me do it."* The something you are speaking about is the Holy Spirit trying to help you.

The Holy Spirit is trying to talk to you, and you keep giving credit to something other than God. It wasn't "a sense." It was the Holy Spirit telling you, *"Run, run, get away from them, this will be a problem..."* That was the Holy Spirit trying to talk to you.

Have you ever had that gut feeling but couldn't define it? But later realized it was a blessing that you obeyed that feeling? My mother would say, *"Jomo, something is not right about them (him or her). I don't know what it is, but something is not right."* That was the Holy Spirit, but she didn't know it.

Psalms 37:23 says, *"The steps of a good and righteous man are directed and established by the Lord and he delights in his way blessing his path."*

Another translation says, *"He busies his way..."* So, as you're walking, God is establishing things, and that's why it's so critical that you receive and listen to what the Holy Spirit's trying to tell you now.

Let's look at what **Romans 9:1** says: ***"I'm telling you the truth in Christ, I'm not lying, my conscience testifies with the enlightened prompting by the Spirit."***

So, your conscience allows the Holy Spirit to talk to you. In this verse, you see how the Holy Spirit flows and connects to disseminate information to your spirit. The Bible says Spirit bears witness with spirit in **Romans 8:16**.

Romans 8:16 (AMP)

[16] ***The Spirit Himself testifies and confirms together with our spirit [assuring us] that we [believers] are children of God***

4 Steps to The Holy Spirit Connecting to Our Thought

    Step 1: The Holy Spirit speaks

    Step 2: The Holy Spirit connects with our spirit

    Step 3: Our spirit connects with our conscience

    Step 4: Our conscience connects with our thoughts

As a pastor, people often ask me about feeling a certain way about a decision they must make or an action they have to take.

They say, "**Pastor, what should I do about this? I feel like I shouldn't do it**." I then ask them the question, "**Does this feeling line up with the things of God?**" We can discern that your feeling is the Holy Spirit trying to communicate with you. God gives you a word, and then you say, "**Man, what do you think?**" Or they may say, *"I think God's telling me to do this. What do you think?"*

And my answer is always "Obey God."

Look at this: "**My conscience testifies with me, and I'm enlightened and prompted by the Spirit**." So, when your conscience tells you to back away, that's the Holy Spirit trying to talk to you. Now, are you going to receive the message?

A guy who has been dating for a while may think she is the one. In that case, I would ask him, "**Did God tell you?**" If God told you that, then I would come into agreement with you. If God didn't say it, it's just your issue and yours to deal with.

In my marriage, we try to be in alignment with all our big decisions. I can't just do what I feel without God's confirmation. Most impulsive decisions I've made without Godly counsel have not gone well. When I was younger, I would say things like, **"You know what? I'm going to start a business!"**

We've done travel business, mortgage business, Amway, Melaleuca, and many others. We have invested in a little bit of everything. We had a garage full of these products that had never been sold. Anybody else got it, too? Yeah, it worked for everybody but us. So now, when my conscience tells me something, I just... I trust it.

Alright, back to **John 16**.
Look at what it says: "*He will glorify and honor me because He, the Holy Spirit will take from what is mine and will disclose it to you.*"

Now, you will start getting revelations about things people don't know.

We were at the first church on Dixon Drive, and we were there for maybe nine months, and we heard the song *Rain On Us*. When it rained, it really rained on us. They had some roof issues, and they also had air conditioning issues, to God be the glory. You can imagine having 250 people in a small room with no air conditioning. I just said, "*Lord, show me a better way. I don't want to be here.*"

Within a few weeks, the pastor I was renting from said, "*I need to talk to you.*" I invited Dr. Pyrtle, a board member and a great friend, to the meeting to make sure I heard clearly. And I said, "*Dr. Pyrtle, I want you to come with me because I sense the pastor wants to throw me out.*" So I went to the meeting, and he said, "*Pastor Jomo, you got to go.*" So, I said, "*You know I paid the agreed amount on time.*" He said, "*You prosper too much. You prosper too much.*"

"Okay, I prosper too much," I said. I then asked, *"How much time do I have before I have to go?"* He said, *"As soon as possible!"*

"Okay..." I said this because God had already told me I was going to be put out.

Sometimes, you have to get put out to be put in position. Sometimes, you have to be fired to be hired. In this faith walk, God has to sometimes push us out of the comforts of the nest so we can soar like an eagle. Much like a mother eagle pushes her babies out of the nest, with the option of falling or flying. We cannot allow negativity and rejection to stop us because, often, that is the birthing place of success.

Wisdom Keys

Number One: Jesus listened to the Spirit

Matthew 4:1 (AMP) *Then Jesus was led by the [Holy] Spirit into the wilderness to be tempted by the devil.*

Matthew 4:1: *Then Jesus was led by who?*

So if Jesus had to be led by the Holy Spirit, what's the likelihood you might need to be led by the Holy Spirit? Now the revelation of the Scripture will bless you.

He was led into the wilderness, not the wealthy place, not the healing place. He was led into a tough place. Not every tough season God allows you to go through is of the devil. Some tough seasons were God saying it's time for promotion. God's breakthrough is locked up in obstacles, and if you can figure out your obstacle, there's a promotion attached to it. So if you're in the midst of a test right now, just pass the test and get your promotion. Stop crying, stop complaining about it, and just pass the test.

By the way, if you don't pass the test, He's a good God. It's going to come back again and again. Now the question is, how many *I's* do you have over your life? Pastor what is a I? If you have been to college, you may know that an "I" means incomplete. It means you have taken the class but have not completed the assignments. So, instead of giving you an F for failure, they give you an I. Some of us got an "I" in the giving, an "I" in patience, and an "I" in love. We need to start fixing these "I's in our lives.

Pass your test, please. Start loving somebody. Forgive them, please. You've got to grow. To grow, you have to let it go. And to live again, we must forgive again.

Number Two: We've got to allow it

Romans 8:14: *"For all who are <u>allowing</u> themselves to be led by the Spirit of God are the sons of God."*

You've got to allow it. You are deciding to follow the prompts of

God. I wonder if you ever had a fight with your conscience; by the way, we do it all time. God tells you to buy someone lunch: *"I'm good, God, I don't want to deal with them."*

My wife had to go to a doctor last week, and a nurse was really helpful. The Holy Spirit said to me, *"Give her $20."* Now, I didn't have to give her anything for doing her job. But the Holy Spirit said, *"Jomo, give her $20."* So, as she was helping my wife, I kind of put it in her pocket, and she said, *"Praise the Lord."* Too many people respond by saying, *"No, I'm good. No, I'm good."* You should keep yourself in a position to receive from a good God. It's not just about you receiving the blessing but not blocking the giver from their blessing.

I believe spirit-led giving is one of the ways God prepares us for our next season in life. God sees you right now in a blessed season, and He will prompt you to do a random act of kindness. *"Prompt? What does that mean?"* He'll give you an inclination, a feeling to give something, but you might say, *"My season is so good right now. I'm good. I don't need to do anything."* God will prompt you in this season for a harvest in the next because God sees you in a future season with nothing on your tree. And you will be hurting, but you don't know it yet. And based on the obedient decision to sow a seed in the good season, you have prepared to receive in your harvest season. So, when you get prompted to buy somebody lunch, think of it as a down payment for your child's lunch because everything you do comes back to you in greater kind.

I remember we were in the process of building our first church. I was driving down the road, going to look at another church, and the Spirit of God told me to pay the mortgage for another pastor's church. I heard, *"**Pay the mortgage.**"* First, you kind of get a little emotional, so I stopped because I didn't know how much the mortgage was. I said, "***Okay, Lord, paying the church mortgage doesn't have anything to do with me.***" If you're like me, you start asking God questions.

"It's not my church. How is it going to help me, Lord?"

"What are you trying to tell me to do, Lord?"

So I said, "***Okay.***" I wrestled for about a day and then said, "***Okay.***" I told my wife. I said, "***Babe, I think God is telling me to pay their first mortgage payment.***"

So, I texted the pastor of that church because, you know, when you don't want to talk about it, you send a text. I didn't want to have a conversation about anything. I just wanted to know the number. I asked, *"**What is the monthly payment?**"* He texted back, *"**$8,454.00**."* I gladly paid for it because it was far less than I expected. Remember, God will never ask you for what you don't have.

I listen to the prompts of God because I don't know what projects God is going to have for me in the future. And I know God is faithful to those who are obedient because His word states, "***God will give me a hundredfold return on the seed.***"

(*Matthew 13:8*) That seed may harvest a new building. The Bible puts it this way, *"What you make happen for others, God will make happen for you" (Eph. 6:8)*, so the quickest way to get to where you want to go is to help somebody get there. If you're led by the Spirit, obey the Spirit. Whatever God asks of you, you got it. You just don't want to give it.

It's critical that I hear His voice. I don't want to do anything without hearing God's voice, can't do it. Once you make the connection your life will never be the same.

My wife and I were in a debate about GPS apps on our phones. I had my navigation app, and she had hers. And we'd be in the car driving somewhere, and both of our apps would be talking at the same time. I wouldn't listen to hers because she thought hers was better, and I would focus on mine because I thought the opposite. All of a sudden, she starts getting traffic updates and police officer updates, and I don't hear anything from my app. Her app then says, "There's a car on the side of the road." I'm looking, hearing nothing from my app, and she says, *"Jomo, why don't you just get my app?"*

In my head, I was thinking,
If I get the app on my phone, that means that I'm wrong and she's right (and I don't want to receive that right now).

I was doing me, so I continued driving with two apps, her app giving real-time updates and my dead app saying nothing. If you think of the GPS systems as God's voice, what kind of God would you prefer, a talking God or a silent God?

One day, I finally put her app on my phone, and it was awesome. I tell you, pride can be a blessing blocker and cause you to ignore the voice of God. I had access to it the whole time but refused it. Our pride limits the Holy Spirit's activity in our lives. Don't allow your ignorance to block God's best for you.

I love this poem on Pride.

Pride – "My Name is Pride" poem by Beth Moore

My name is Pride. I am a cheater.

I cheat you of your God-given destiny...

because you demand your own way.

I cheat you of contentment...

because you "deserve better than this."

I cheat you of knowledge...

because you already know it all.

I cheat you of healing...

because you are too full of you to forgive.

I cheat you of holiness...

because you refuse to admit when you are wrong.

I cheat you of vision...

because you'd rather look in the mirror than out a window.

I cheat you of genuine friendship...

because nobody's going to know the real you.

I cheat you of love...

because real romance demands sacrifice.

I cheat you of greatness in heaven...

because you refuse to wash another's feet on earth.

I cheat you of God's glory...

because I convinced you to seek your own.

My name is Pride. I am a cheater.

You like me because you think I'm always looking out for you.

Untrue.

I'm looking to make a fool of you.

God has so much for you, I admit, but don't worry...

If you stick with me you'll never know.

I realize now that my wife's GPS app was better and a more trusted voice than mine. It's amazing to me how we can trust the voice of a GPS system and not trust God who has the best GPS system. And it's not a global positioning system; it's God's positioning system.

I close with this: I was reading a story about a young girl. She was a quarter-miler runner in a 400-meter race, and the man was watching the race. He saw the girl get in her stance, but she had an earpiece in her ear, so he just watched the race with the girl with the earpiece in her ear. But as he watched, he saw a man on the side of the race running along and talking. At the end of the race, the man running along with the young girl runs over and hugs her. So, the man watching was curious to find out what the earpiece was all about. The man, who was the young girl's father, says, "*My daughter's blind, and every race I speak in her ear. So, as she goes around the corner, I'm saying, 'you're hitting the curve right now, baby, start turning, start turning, start turning*." A reporter then asks the young girl, "*How can you run a quarter mile and be blind, not knowing if certain things are happening?*" She says, "*I've learned to trust the voice. He's never led me wrong.*"

Question: Have you trusted His voice?

He'll never lead you wrong. There are so many times in life you knew not to do it, but you did it. Brothers and sisters, God is still speaking, and you've got to trust the voice.

Let's Pray

Father God, I thank You for Your Word. Yes, God, I pray your Word hit its mark. Lord, I pray we trust Your voice, for Your Word says you're not a man that You shall lie nor the son of man that you shall repent. Lord, your words say, "*My sheep know my voice, a stranger they will not follow*." Lord, I thank you today for hearing your voice. Speak to us, Holy Spirit, order our steps. Lord, we're sick and tired of ourselves. We want Your will, not our will, Your way, not our way. Less of us, more of you in Jesus name, Amen.

Questions

1. Do you have a good relationship with the Holy Spirit?

2. How do you know when the Holy Spirit is speaking to you?

3. Have you ever seen your conscience and the Holy Spirit work together?

4. What are the 4 Steps to The Holy Spirit Connecting to Our Thoughts?

5. Can you remember a time when God gave you clear instructions, and you obeyed and prospered?

6. Can you remember a time when it looked bad, but God worked it together for you?

7. Have you ever had a time you listened to God, and it led to a hard season?

8. Name a time when you struggled to listen to God.

9. Can you name a time when pride blinded you from hearing God's voice?

Chapter Six

Situations and Circumstances

God will use every tool imaginable to get a message to His children. And there will be times in our lives when words don't seem to get our attention. At those times, God will place us in situations and circumstances that will do it. Some will view these moments as obstacles instead of opportunities. If we are believers, we must believe what **Romans 8:28** tells us: "...***All things work together for [our] good.***" So, instead of complaining about things, we must reframe our minds to see them as divine appointments.

Let me share a story about comment cards received by Bridger Wilderness, a national park in the state of Wyoming. This park is well known for its mountainous terrain and steep hiking trails. These are actual comments that some visitors left:

"Trails need to be wider so people can walk while they hold hands."

"Trails need to be reconstructed. "

"Please avoid building trails that go uphill."

"Too many bugs, leeches, spiders, and spider webs."

"Please spray the wilderness to get rid of areas with these pests."

"Please pave the hills so that they can be snow plowed during the winter."

"Chair lifts need to be on some of the places so I can see the view."

"Coyotes made too much noise last night and kept me awake. Please eradicate these annoying animals."

"Small deer came into my camp last night and stole my jar of pickles. Is there any way I can get reimbursed?"

"Reflectors need to be placed on trees every 50 feet so I can see at night."

"Escalators would help on these steep hills."

"A McDonald's would be good at the top of the hill."

"The places where trails do not exist are not well marked."

"Too many rocks on the mountain."

These are real comments sent to a national park! A national park in Wyoming!

The truth is, we're not fond of pain or any slight discomfort. We rebel at the suggestion, recoil at the sight of it, and reject the idea that it might be good for us. Life lessons are almost always taught in the classroom of suffering, heartache, and pain. This is where we usually learn our best lessons.

When trials and tribulations come, we often ask ourselves four questions:

1. *"Is God putting me through a test?"*
2. *"Is this the wages of my sin? / Am I reaping what I've sown?"*
3. *"Is the devil attacking me?"*
4. *"Am I being persecuted for being righteous?"*

Now, when you're going through something, make sure you do a check-up from the neck up—the problem could be you! It could also be God allowing you to go through a test, as He did with Job. Since tests are a part of life, make sure you benefit from them by learning the lessons they offer. Come out smarter! Come out stronger! Make the tough times count!

The good news is that the four questions have four simple solutions:

1. *If the unfolding situation is a test from the Lord, then pass it!*

2. *If you're reaping what you've sown, then repent!*

3. **If the attack is from the enemy, then resist!**

4. **If you are being persecuted for being in the right standing with God, then endure it!**

    A great example of this is when Jesus told the disciples to go to the other side, and he would meet them there. It was to their dismay that they found themselves in the middle of a storm. They were following instructions and the instructions led them into a faith fight. (Matthew 14:22-33) The question we must ask is, "Why?" Jesus was testing their faith. Remember, not every negative situation is connected to disobedience. It could be that God wants to promote you.

In our faith walk, God will allow us to go through certain seasons or situations to get our attention. I felt the Holy Spirit tell me that God wanted me to be a preacher. I said, **"Lord, no! I don't want to be a preacher. I don't want any of that! I'm a good motivational speaker. I make good money, and I'm not going to do it, Lord!"** Then I thought about it and said, **"Ok, Lord. When I have saved enough money, then I'll become a pastor!"** To be clear, I had no problem serving God because I was already serving Him by being an assistant pastor. I just wrestled with the idea of having to ask people for money. I also didn't want to deal with the judgment that might come from people thinking I needed them. I know, I know, but that was *my* struggle! Then, out of nowhere, came a storm. I remember it like it was yesterday....

I was on my way to a business trip in Los Angeles. I had eight speaking engagements poised to net me around $40,000.00. As soon as I landed in LA, my phone started vibrating nonstop. All of the calls were cancellations from the events we had scheduled! EVERYWHERE cancelled!

I was blown away. With our newly cleared schedules, my business partner and I decided to go to Red Robin for some food. Now, I know Red Robin is new to us on the *East* Coast, but they've been popular on the West Coast for a long time! While we were enjoying our bottomless french fries and strawberry lemonades—that lemonade is straight from Jesus, by the way—my partner said to me, *"Bro, I think God is telling you it's time."* He said, "*Jonah, I think you need to get off the ship. Otherwise, we are all going to die!*" Now, he knew my name was not Jonah...

For perspective, let me give you the Bible CliffsNotes version of the Jonah story. Jonah was a prophet that God sent to a town named Nineveh to warn people about changing their wicked ways. Jonah decided to disobey God's orders and went AWOL (Absent Without Leave). He fled from his assignment and God's presence by boarding a ship he wasn't supposed to be on. So, God sent storms to ravage the ship, bit by bit, until the men realized that Jonah's presence was the reason for their troubles. His disobedience was about to cost many men their lives and their cargo. They threw Jonah overboard, and the storm stopped. Jonah got swallowed by a whale and spent three days there praying and reconsidering his assignment. Once the whale spat him out on the shores of Nineveh, Jonah wasted no time doing what God told him to do.

Well! After my business partner called *me* Jonah, that was all it took! Shortly after we returned home, we signed the necessary paperwork to dissolve our partnership. It was then that I realized that God had to close every door in order for me to follow Him. What we call a closed door, God calls a change of direction. If God waits for us to make decisions, we may never do certain things. So, sometimes, God has to get extreme. He's got to fire us, demote us, or kick our butts out so He can push us into our destiny. God has to allow certain situations and circumstances to happen so He can get our attention. He will even put us into uncomfortable situations to get us alone so we can hear Him better.

"Can you hear me now?"

My father used to say, *"You have two options, son; you can listen, or you can feel! Either way, you're gonna do it!"* Remember, God will allow things to happen as a way of saying, *"Hello, I need to talk to you! I need some time with you."*

As I look back on this season, God tried to tell me personally, then he had people try to tell me, then problems came, and after the problems came the pain.

The Bible spoke of a brother named Paul. He was shipwrecked

three times. He'd been beaten and scourged; he went through everything, but through it all, Paul received some major revelations.

2 Corinthians 12:7-10 (AMP)
"Because of the surpassing greatness and extraordinary nature of the revelations [which I received from God], for this reason, to keep me from thinking of myself as important, a thorn in the flesh was given to me, a messenger of Satan, to torment and harass me—to keep me from exalting myself!"

I want to make sure you caught that. Paul said, "a messenger of Satan," which means God can use even the Devil for our good. I believe one of the mistakes many believers make is that they think Satan and God are on the same level. That's a fallacy. Satan is subject to God. Satan only operates with the authority that was released to him from Adam. More details on this can be found in chapters 1 and 2 of Job, where you will see that God summoned his sons (angels), and Satan showed up and had to answer to God, too! I believe that's why it's so critical that you have ingrained in your mind **Romans 8:28**, which tells *us that all things are working together for the good for those who love God and those who are called according to his purpose, plan, and design*. Though some things may not feel good, you must trust that the situation will work out for your good eventually.

Why is it that when everything is good, some stop listening to God and giving Him thanks, but when our money is funny, and our change is strange, we suddenly seem more apt to hear Him?

Suddenly, we begin to sing the song, *"...I need Thee, every hour, I need thee."* Why don't we need Him when stuff is going well in our lives?

The Bible tells us that Paul went through many trials, but each trial came with a revelation. We are no different from Paul! God has allowed some of us to be broke so that you would understand that He is Jehovah Jireh - Your Provider. God allows us to be sick so that we would know that He is Jehovah Rapha - your Healer. God will remind us of who He is by allowing us to go through various seasons in life. He is the great "I Am," so when you're not listening, God will create a situation or circumstance as if to say:

"...Can you hear Me now?"

In my journey, I have learned that the pits of life will provide what I like to call "proper perspective-producing power." Let me explain. Sometimes we must experience going broke and then getting a little bit of money to develop a different appreciation for money. The pit you were in gave you space and time to think and change your perspective.

If you can find the purpose in your pain, you will find your power. God doesn't allow you to just go through things for "fun." His goal in allowing you to go through something is for you to learn from it. Remember this: you are not just going through something but *growing* through something!

In January 2015, I was diagnosed with stage III colon cancer. I asked God, *"Why? What did I do to deserve this?"* I wasn't any different from most people in my position; I threw myself a good ol' why-me-themed pity party! But as I did laps around the hospital after being laid up post-surgery, God said, *"Son, I put you in the hospital because you needed to rest/slow down."* Then, I had to go for chemotherapy at the cancer center. While I sat there, God showed me many things, things I might have missed had I not been forced to sit down and rest.

Please don't wait for trials to come before you stop to listen to God because He will slow you down whether you want to or not. It's much better for you to make some time for Him so that He doesn't have to clear your calendar. And believe me, He *will* clear your schedule!

Once that started to sink in with me, I resigned to His will and said, *"Okay, Lord, I receive! I need to rest more. Okay, I finally got it. Okay, what else?"* I made some adjustments to my life because God *made* me listen. Sometimes, we must hit rock bottom before we listen. We walk around trying to convince everyone that we're all good, but God will allow some things to hit our life, and suddenly, we change our perspective.

2 Corinthians 12:8 (AMP)
"Concerning this <u>I pleaded with the Lord three times</u> that it might leave me;"

In this verse, Paul clearly begged God to remove his thorn three times. Of course, we know that God said no each time. Have you ever asked God to remove something from your life that would not budge? *"Lord, please, Lord, please take him away! Lord, take her away! Lord, please let this child leave this house. Lord, please let my sister and brother-in-law find their own place! Lord, Jesus!"* Yet, God continues to say, "*No, I've got to keep you in a certain position because when you're in this position, you're more fruitful.*"

Let me give you another example. When we started erecting our first building, I had a figure in my head of how much I thought we should spend. Even though I wasn't clear on what the final cost would be, I was clear that I did not want to have a 20-year building fund to get it done. Anybody who's ever built a building from scratch knows that unseen variables always come into play. One of ours was the turtles! Not just any ol' run-of-the-mill turtles, but special gopher turtles! Yup, special gopher turtles that needed to be removed carefully and placed in a sanctuary. We called the only company licensed to move gopher turtles. *The only one!* That lovely, specialized company offered to move each turtle for $1,400.00 per turtle! I almost fell out! *"Lord, why?!"* That's all I could say. God replied, *"Jomo, you were moving too fast! Don't sacrifice My vision for your budget!"* You see, God doesn't see our budget! I was looking at the budget and started to take things off the building, so God told me to slow down! We ended up at an overall cost of $3.2 million, and it was fully paid off!

The truth is, at times, we all downsize what God shows us to meet our limited budgets. We know what God showed us, but we still try to minimize things to match our bad math. Guess what? Our math will never add up to God's! And guess what else? If God calls us to something, we will never be able to complete it using our own abilities. God's going to remind us that we're going to have to trust Him. We'll have to believe Him even when things make no sense.

God put me in a series of situations to slow my fast butt down. I told God, *"Look, I'm not a preacher. The NFL didn't work out like I thought it would, but I'm a speaker now. I'm balling again! I'm making good money, got my S-500, I'm following the Lord, I've got five properties now, and I already told Charmaine that by 35, I'd be a millionaire. I'm buying one property a year, and eventually, I'll have ten properties..."* I had all my plans laid out, and God just said, *"No, you're going to be my servant."*

Have you ever had a plan that you thought was great and had God just say no? I had plans, but then God kicked my plans to the curb. I kept trying to negotiate with Him and tell him who I thought I was. "*I'm a storyteller! I know how to tell good stories, but Lord, I don't have the heavy, reverend-style breathing thing down yet. Are you sure you want me?!*"

God knew exactly who I was and what He wanted me to do; every gift and talent was innate in me for His call. God will take you through whatever He has to take you through to get you to where He wants you to be. And for many of us, it comes through trial and tribulation.

Let's jump back into the Word.

2 Corinthians 12:9 (AMP)
"But He said to me, "My grace is sufficient for you. My loving kindness and my grace are more than enough, always available, regardless of the situation for my power is being perfected and completed and shows itself most effectively in your weakness. Therefore I will all the more gladly boast in my weakness so that the power of Christ may completely enfold me and may dwell in me."

Look what The Message Bible says: *"My grace is enough. It's all you need. My strength comes into its own in your weakness."*

Once I heard that, I was glad to let it happen. I quit focusing on the handicap and began appreciating my gift. We see God telling us, *"Stop focusing on your negatives and focus on your positives."* He will work with whatever you bring to Him. It doesn't have to be fancy. You just must have faith.

When I started preaching, I tried to be like other pastors I watched. Man, my voice was gone! My voice was sore. I was an all-around mess. God said, *"Jomo, you were fearfully and wonderfully made in my image, in my likeness, and I put a gift on the inside of you, do not be intimidated; do not be discouraged; do not be dismayed for what I have for you is for you and the Bible says a man's gift will make room for him and bring him before great men. You have to understand that you were gifted and talented before there was ever a gifted and talented."*

God put gifts and talents inside of us. If we could be who God has called us to be, He has already made room for us. The challenge is we want to be second-rate Beyonces' or Jay-Zs instead of just being our original selves. You've got to make up your mind that God has a place for you, and you do not have to compare your situation to anyone else's situation or circumstance. God has prepared a place for you as Psalms says, *"He's prepared a table in the presence of my enemies"* (Psalms 23:5 AMP)

Sometimes, God puts you into situations and circumstances to remind you, *"I still got you. Don't look at where others are in the race; just look at where I brought you from."* We are often so concerned about what other people are doing versus what God is doing in us. Look where God brought you from and look where you are today. You can celebrate right there!

The enemy of your life wants you to focus on your handicap, focus on what you don't do well, what you don't do right. Your gift will make room for you. Your gift will take you to your wealthy place. Just tap into what God has given you.

Look at **Philippians 2:13 (AMP)**: *"For it is not your strength, but it is God who is effectively at work in you both to will and to* *work, that is to strengthen, energizing and creating in you the longing and the ability to fulfill your purpose.*

Stop trying to figure out how you will do it. God says, "*I'm going to give you the power, the ability to fulfill your purpose, so all you have to do is show up.*" We have won half of the battle just by being in position. Don't care what they say about you or your past. God has put something special inside of you. You are fully equipped, all you need to do is put yourself in the right atmosphere, and you will blossom. God will use you, but you must get past you. Our biggest challenge is we don't believe we qualify. You don't believe you're good enough. Well, guess what? I was the same way.

When I was a teen, I worked at a place named Discovery Zone in Maryland, which was very similar to Chuck E Cheese. I was a big kid at heart and had lots of fun with the guests; the owner recognized this in me and asked me to host the children's birthday parties. This meant I had to make an announcement on the PA system for each party. Now, I was not the best reader, so I struggled. I mean, I struggled big time to the point I was fearful of speaking in public. So, I went to some other workers and made a deal; I would clean their rooms if they made the announcement for me. I was so scared to be on the intercom, sounding crazy, that I was willing to clean and pay someone else. Today, I speak in public daily—fear gone!

Your greatest victory will come after you deal with your greatest fear which may be devil-induced to keep you out of purpose.

Let's go back to our text, **Philippians 2:13 (AMP)**
"For it's not in your strength but it is God who is effectively at work..." Both will and to work that is strengthening you, energizing and creating in you the longing and the ability to fulfill whose purpose?

You need to surrender and say, **"Lord do what you got to do. I'm available to you, Father. Use me any way you like."** When you do that, everything will start changing. You must take your hands off the steering wheel. You must give God control. He knows what He wants to do. You must have faith and allow Him to use you.

Let's go back to 2 Corinthians 12:10 (AMP)

"Because I am well pleased with my weaknesses, the stresses, with persecutions, with difficulties for the sake of Christ, for when I am weak in human strength then I am strong, truly powerful, truly drawing from God's strength."

The Message Bible translates, **"It was for the case of Christ's strength moving in my weakness. Now I take my limitations in stride with good cheer, these limitations that cut me down to size—abuse, accidents, oppositions, bad breaks. I just let Christ take over. So the weaker I get, the stronger I become.**

We must learn how to walk with our weaknesses, trusting that God is with us. And if God is for us, who can be against us?

(Romans 8:31)

Wisdom Key

Number One: God speaks through experience

Deuteronomy 8:3-4 (AMP)
³He humbled you and allowed you to be hungry and fed you with manna, [a substance] which you did not know, nor did your fathers know, so that He might make you understand [by personal experience] that man does not live by bread alone, but man lives by every word that proceeds out of the mouth of the Lord.

God sometimes must break us down to position us to be built back up. God said, *"Look, if you think it's about your job, your career, or your business, I'm going to take it all away until you get back on track. This should be your focus. If you take care of this, I'll take care of everything else; your marriage, your kids, everything else.*

Now, why is it that we can understand disciplining our children, but when God wants to discipline us, we take it personally? I'm sure you have heard the saying, "If you don't listen, you are going to feel." So, God says, *" Look, I'll make you hungry if you don't want to listen."* Hungry people are good listeners.

Number Two: God speaks when we're at the end of the rope

Matthew 5:3-5 (MSG)
3 "You're blessed when you're at the end of your rope. With less of you there is more of God and his rule.

When you're at the end of your rope, all you have is God. Some of you reading this today are there, and you're just holding on. But when you're at the end of your rope, you're at the beginning of God. When you're at the end of your rope, you can't afford to hold on to unnecessary things. All you've got is Him. Guess what? That's where God wants you.

Hebrews 11:6 implies *unless we're living with the possibility of failure, we're not pleasing Him*, meaning we are to be constantly pressing our faith. When was the last time you did something big for God? When was the last time you stepped out and said, *" I don't know how it's going to work out. I'm just going to trust God."*

We must understand that when we are at the end of us, we are at the beginning of Him. "*Not my will, Father, Your will. Not my way Father, Your way*." Some of us are so comfortable we've stopped trusting God.

I was reading about a man. He was climbing up a cliff, and his rope snapped. He was left hanging off the cliff. He yelled, "*Is there anybody up there?*" No reply.
"*Help! Is there anybody up there?*"
A voice says, "*I'm here.*"
"*Who are you?*"
"*I'm God.*"

"Who?"

"God."

"Can you help me?"

"Absolutely. All you have to do is let go."

Long pause.

"Is there anybody else?"

I close with this great message I read:

I asked for strength, and God gave me difficulties to make me strong.

I asked for wisdom, and God gave me problems to solve.

I asked for prosperity, and God gave me a brain and brawn to work.

I asked for courage, and God gave me dangers to overcome.

I asked for patience, and God placed me in situations where I was forced to wait.

I asked for love, and God gave me troubled people to help.

I asked for favors, and God gave me opportunities.

I received nothing I wanted.

I received everything I needed.

Often, what you ask God for will be masked in a problem, and if you figure it out, you get a promotion. We must stop complaining about our season and just say, *"Lord, what am I supposed to learn from this?"*

6 Keys to Help You Discover God's Vision for Your Life

1. His Word

2. Inward witness-gut feeling

3. Your pastor- Godly leader

4. Agreement from credible others

5. Circumstances will align themselves with the Vision or the Word

6. Family- those who have grown with you and know you

Questions

1. What questions should you ask yourself when you are in a challenging situation?

2. How do you handle your challenges when they arise?

3. What doors in your life has God closed that you were not ready for Him to close?

4. How do you handle the disappointment of God changing your course?

5. What fears are holding you back?

6. Name a circumstance when you learned that God was helping you, not hurting you in a situation.

Chapter Seven

Keys To Discerning The Voice

In this chapter, we will see how Simon Peter accessed greater grace by aligning his spirit with the Holy Spirit. And with this connection, his ability to hear changed. Jesus recognized this and gave him a name change to Peter. And with the name change came access to the keys to the kingdom. Our ability to hear right is the gateway to greater things in the kingdom. We will live on the level that we can hear and obey.

We're going to teach from **Matthew 16:13-23 (AMP)**
"Now when Jesus went into the region of Caesarea Philippi, he asked his disciples, "Who do people say the son of man is?" And they answered, "Some say John the Baptist, others say Elijah, and still others say Jeremiah, or just one of the prophets." And he said to them, "But who do you say I am?"

Now, this is a test in which Jesus asks them, ***"Who am I to you?"*** Jesus understood that if they didn't recognize who He was, they could not receive all He had to give them. Jesus is saying, ***"I know what they're saying, but what do you say?"***

John 10:27 (AMP) shows us the connection between hearing and obeying God's voice.

"The sheep that are my own hear my voice and listen to me, I know them and they follow me."

Quick point here: notice it says *"... my own sheep,"* meaning that there are other sheep. For Him to say, *"my voice"* implies there must be other voices that can be heard. *"I know them and they follow me..."* So when Jesus asked the question, *"Who do you say I am?"* he wanted to get it answered.

Matthew 16:16-17 (AMP), *Simon Peter replied, <u>"You are the Christ (the Messiah, the Anointed)</u>, the Son of the living God."* *17 Then Jesus answered him, "Blessed [happy, spiritually secure, favored by God] are you, Simon son of Jonah, because flesh and blood (mortal man) did not reveal this to you, but My Father who is in heaven.*

Simon Peter replied in **Matthew 16:16 (AMP),** *"You are the Christ, the Messiah, the Anointed, the Son of the Living God."*

Then Jesus says,

"Blessed [happy, spiritually secure, favored by God] are you, Simon son of Jonah, <u>because flesh and blood (mortal man) did not reveal this to you, but My Father who is in heaven</u>.

Jesus blessed him for getting it right. I believe the Holy Spirit had to be working with Simon Peter. Jesus' next statement implies that Simon Peter got it. He says, *"Flesh and blood did not reveal this to you but Father."*

I want to remind you of something from a previous chapter. Let's look at **Romans 9:1 (AMP)** *"I'm telling you the truth in Christ, I'm not lying. My conscience testifies with me enlightened and prompted by my spirit..."*

Let me explain the connection here. Simon Peter got his understanding through his conscience working with the Holy Spirit. It's critical that you understand that our conscience is working in connection with the Holy Spirit. When we fight our conscience, we're really fighting the Spirit of God, trying to push us in the right direction.

Once Jesus identified that Simon Peter heard the right voice, look what He gave him.

Matthew 16:18 (AMP)

And I say to you that <u>you are Peter</u>, and on this rock I will build My church; and the gates of Hades (death) will not overpower it [by preventing the resurrection of the Christ].

Notice right before this verse, we called him Simon Peter. Now in this verse, his name is changed. Let me explain what this means. The word "Simon" means "Shaky" or "Pebble." Peter means "Rock." So when Jesus first spoke to him, Simon Peter, he said, *"Shaky, rock."*

For context, we have days when our faith is strong, and some days, our faith is shaky. One day you say, *"I feel great! Glory to*

God!" The next day they say, *"Oh Lord glory!"* We go back and forth and vacillate, much like Simon Peter. We sometimes are unstable in our faith. But Jesus says, *"I need to speak to the rock in you, the solid part in you."* Jesus then says, *"I now say to you, you are Peter."* But wasn't he Peter before? Why would Jesus declare it if he wasn't already Peter? Because Peter had been shaky.

After Peter answered the question correctly, it triggered a gateway of power and authority. Notice that after Jesus calls him Peter, he gives him the keys to the kingdom. I believe Jesus would not have released this without knowing that Peter could hear from God.

Matthew 16: 19 (AMP)

I will give you the keys (authority) of the kingdom of heaven; and whatever you bind [forbid, declare to be improper and unlawful] on earth will have [already] been bound in heaven, and whatever you loose [permit, declare lawful] on earth will have[already] been loosed in heaven.

God is telling Peter now that he knows who he is, he can have the keys. Now that Peter has accepted who he is, he now has access. He now has a new name, and God has opened the door for his next level of anointing. We are not waiting on God; God is waiting for us to recognize and understand who He is, which will, in turn, help us understand who we are. We often forget who we are, but God never forgets who we are. We were created in His image and His likeness. Therefore, He knows our true name and everything that we are capable of!

You have to tell yourself:

I was fearfully and wonderfully made in God's image and God's likeness. I'm the head and not the tail. I'm blessed coming in. I'm blessed coming out. No weapon formed against me shall prosper. I am more than a conqueror. My latter shall be greater, weeping may endure for a night, but joy cometh in the morning time. I always win. God got my back."

People are often discouraged and depressed because they keep focusing on who they are not. If you can focus on who you are in Christ Jesus, everything will be different. God made you; therefore, you're not junk. For whatever God made is gifted and talented.

God can't take you to the level that He desires without us being able to understand when He's talking to us. God's will already exist, and the Spirit will give you a revelation of things that are to be done. The Spirit will speak to those who have ears to hear. The Spirit echoes the will of God for us.

In **Matthew 16:19 (AMP)**, God is making it clear that we have the power to bind and loose with our words. The key to our ability for binding and loosing is tied to hearing from Him properly. For when we hear from Him properly, we will speak properly. We end up becoming an echo of God's will on Earth. His will becomes our will through us properly hearing and interpreting His voice which comes from His Word. As the book of **Numbers** states, God's word does not change, meaning His will does not change.

Numbers 23:19 (KJV) says
"God is not a man that he shall lie nor the Son of Man that he should repent,"

Let's get back to **Matthew 16**,

Matthew 16:20-21 (AMP) says,
"Then he gave the disciples strict orders to tell no one that he was the Christ. From that time on Jesus began to show his disciples telling them He must go to Jerusalem and endure many things at the hands of the elders, chief priests and the scribes and be killed and be raised from the dead, from death on the third day.

We notice here that Jesus began to teach them more as their understanding grew.

[22] Peter took Him aside [to speak to Him privately] and began to reprimand Him, saying, "May God forbid it! This will never happen to You." [23] But Jesus turned and said to Peter, "Get behind Me, Satan! You are a stumbling block to Me; for you are not setting your mind on things of God, but on things of man."

I can imagine Jesus thinking to himself, I just promoted you, and now you're rebuking me! Jesus then tells Peter, **"Get behind me, Satan,"** because He knew that was not Peter talking. He told Peter, **"You listen while I deal with this fool (the devil) over here."** That's why it's critical for you to know God's voice. You see how quickly Jesus dealt with the devil.

Understand the devil is a spirit that needs a body to flow through. Peter didn't realize that going against God's word would create room for the enemy to enter his body and be used against him. That's why it's imperative that you are full of the word of God so that there is no room for anyone else. When you doubt God's word, you become "double-minded," which means you are unstable and shaky in all your ways **(James 1:8)**.

Any person, place, or thing that goes against God's plan and purpose needs to be rebuked, and you should say, **"Get Behind Me, Satan."**

You must know who is speaking to you. I remember there was a time my father and I were having a conversation about me being a speaker. As he spoke in doubt, **"You were always a quiet child. You were not a talkative child,"** I could feel his words start to get to me. I simply whispered, **"Get behind me, Satan,"** because I knew it wasn't my father talking to me but the devil using him.

Our battle is not flesh and blood but spiritual. The enemy speaks through people.

Let's get back to Matthew

Matthew 16:23 (AMP)

"But Jesus turned and said to Peter, "<u>Get behind Me, Satan!</u> You are a stumbling block to Me; <u>for you are not setting your mind on things of God, but on things of man.</u>"

When He says "You" with a capital "Y," He is speaking to the devil. And with the lowercase "y," He is also talking to Peter, who wasn't focused on God's plan. In the verse you saw Jesus dealing with, the spirit realm, and the natural realm in one sentence.

Wisdom Keys

Number One: We must set our minds

Colossians 3:2 (AMP)

<u>Set your mind</u> and keep focused habitually on the things above [the heavenly things], not on things that are on the earth [which have only temporal value].

It is critical that you set your mind on heavenly things and not things that are earthly. Simon Peter got off course because he started thinking personally. You have to be kingdom-minded. Being kingdom-minded means that certain things in your life will suffer, and you'll go through storms, but you must realize that all things work together for good **(Romans 8:28)**.

I thought about when I was going through chemotherapy and having to go to the oncologist and get all these tests done repeatedly. God introduced me to different people, and now I see why God did everything. I took it as a personal indictment of my life versus God just using me. A few nurses who treated me gave their lives to the Lord and joined the church. Could it be that God allowed me to go through that storm to save a soul?

Number Two: We must not put a limit on God

Ephesians 3:20 (AMP)

Now to Him who is able to [carry out His purpose and] do superabundantly more than all that we dare ask or think [infinitely beyond our greatest prayers, hopes, or dreams], according to His power that is at work within us,

Jesus's death and resurrection were so far beyond Peter's thought process he rejected them. You need to have more space in your brain for things you don't understand and then things you know. Just because you don't know how it works doesn't mean it's not effective. You may not know how electricity works, but I bet you won't stick your finger in a socket. Stop limiting God to your ability to believe. If you don't put a limit on God, God won't put a limit on you. It **Isaiah 55:8-9** says, *"My thoughts are not your thoughts nor my ways your ways,"* *says the Lord, for as the heavens are higher than Earth* *so my ways are higher than yours and my thoughts higher than your thoughts."*

Five Filters to Knowing God's Voice

Number 1: Does what I hear line up with God's word? That's the most important part. God's voice is locked in His word; you'll find it in the Word.

Number 2: Is the voice consistent with God's character? Love, wisdom, power, holiness, justice, and truth.

Number 3: Is it being confirmed through messages or a message? Am I hearing it from the church and study groups? It will all line up.

Number 4: Is it beyond me? This is the critical point. Every time God asks me to do something, it seems to stretch me. It's not comfortable. God's word will get you out of your comfort zone. It will push you to a place you don't want to be pushed.

Number 5: Will it please God?

Once you get these things lined up, then you can verify it's God's voice. It seems difficult at first, but the more you spend time with Him, the easier it becomes.

Questions

1. Do you know who you are in Christ Jesus?

2. Why do you think Jesus asked them, "Who do people say who I am?"

3. How does God speak to you?

4. Who has the keys to the kingdom?

5. How do you use the keys to the kingdom?

6. Have you ever witnessed someone speaking to you but not sounding like themself?

7. How did Jesus confront Satan?

8. How do you set your mind on the things of God?

9. What are the filters for God's voice?

Chapter Eight

The Matrix - Visions

In this chapter, we're going to learn about how God uses visions to communicate with us. The Bible speaks of visions and dreams, letting us know there is a distinct difference. I believe visions come while you're conscious or awake, and dreams come while you are asleep. They work together as different forms of communication that God can use to connect with us. I don't believe you have to be asleep for God to speak to you; you just have to be aware. I know in my life, I can get the vision just by being still.

I don't know if you have ever seen the movie, *The Matrix,* but it's a classic with so many subliminal messages. In the movie, Neil, the main character, is called **"The One,"** and they keep asking him, **"Are you the One?"** In the Bible, they ask Jesus the same question in **Matthew 11:3**.

Matthew 11:3 (AMP)
and asked Him, "Are You the Expected One (the Messiah), or should we look for someone else [who will be the promised One]?"

There was a lady called **"Trinity,"** and she was symbolic of the Holy Spirit. They gave Neil a choice to make between a red or blue pill. Some of you may never have watched the movie, but I want you to go back and watch the movie.

In the Matrix, we see two kinds of worlds, those in and out of the matrix. It's a reflection of the two worlds in which we live, the natural and the spiritual. The Bible says we don't fight a natural battle; we fight a spiritual battle (Eph. 6).

12 For our struggle is not against <u>flesh and blood [contending only with physical</u> opponents], but against the rulers, against the powers, against the world forces of this [present] darkness, against the <u>spiritual</u> forces of wickedness in the heavenly (supernatural) places.

Our focus in this chapter will be from **Acts 9.**

1 Now Saul, still breathing threats and murder against the disciples of the Lord [and relentless in his search for believers], went to the high priest,

Now, Saul eventually becomes Paul; after his transformation on Damascus road. At the time that he met Jesus, he was persecuting Christians. Paul's life is a testimony to us that it doesn't matter how jacked up, broken down, or lost we may think we are. God can step in at any time and change our destiny. God can use anybody at any time.

Back into **Acts 9:2-6**
2 and he asked for letters [of authority] from him to the synagogues at Damascus, so that if he found any men or women there belonging to the Way [believers, followers of Jesus the Messiah], men and women alike, he could arrest

them and bring them bound [with chains] to Jerusalem. ³ As he traveled he approached Damascus, and <u>suddenly a light from heaven flashed around him [displaying the glory and majesty of Christ]; ⁴ and he fell to the ground and heard a voice [from heaven] saying to him, "Saul, Saul, why are you persecuting and oppressing Me?"</u> ⁵ And Saul said, "Who are You, Lord?" And He answered, "I am Jesus whom you are persecuting, ⁶ now get up and go into the city, and you will be told what you must do."

Key Point: Jesus doesn't step into a person's life and starts giving them instructions often, so I don't want you to make this your expectation. Of course, God can do it, but we don't see many instances of it in the Bible. I can't say that God audibly speaks to me on a regular basis. There were a few, but I can say He's always trying to connect with me in many forms.

The Bible says He speaks to Saul and says, **"Get up and go."** Often, the biggest struggle we have as believers is that we're trying to ask God why we should go when He says, **"Get up and go."** Listen, family, faith is total obedience without total understanding. If you are waiting on total understanding, you will miss God. You may have missed your moment by the time it makes sense to you. So I have to be mindful in this faith walk that I must understand and realize with God that it may not make sense, but I have to be obedient.

Those in the armed forces clearly understand this process of taking directions without total understanding. They only receive one order at a time, and once the task is accomplished, they receive the next order. Our faith is displayed in our ability to do what God has asked of us.

Let's go the Acts 9:7

⁷ "The men who were traveling with him were terrified and stood speechless, hearing the voice but seeing no one."

We see from scripture that all heard the voice, but not all could see the vision. God had to recalibrate Saul for his new mission. For all of Saul's life, he dealt with what he saw and then acted. Now, God is going to reconfigure his processor by taking his vision. God will train him to walk by faith, not sight.

In the process of God preparing us for His purposes, we will go through a stripping season, where things are taken away from us. God will break us down to build us up for the new thing He wants to do. We can see that in the lives of biblical heroes.

- God told Abraham to leave his home, family, and all that was familiar to an unknown place.

- Moses had to flee from the home where he was raised.

- Jacob had to flee from his brother Esau.

- Ruth had to go back with Naomi.

- Joseph had to go through a pit, persecution, and prison before the palace.

The process is much like a house renovation. If you have a house with a cracked door, window, wall, or roof, we can fix it; but if the foundation is cracked, the building's condemned. God reconstructed Saul's foundation to become Paul. In life, we get frustrated when God breaks us down. Whether it be a relationship, job, or finances, God is saying, "**I can't build on a cracked foundation.**" It would make no sense for God to put resources into a cracked foundation. When your foundation is cracked, you're jacked. Many of us get frustrated with God because we think He took them away, because the job didn't work out, or our plans didn't work out the way we planned.

God knows the foundation we need to build on. If you ever have a chance to study building structures, you will learn that you can only go as high as you go deep. So if God wants you to go high in Him, you're going to have to get deep with Him. When we were constructing our first building, we had to wait a little longer than we wanted to put the steel beams up because we didn't have the right PSI. The pressure was not at the right density to support the weight of the building.

Could God be waiting for you to develop the right density in your foundation to build on?

So, God took away Saul's vision for a season. He was blind and being led by the hand, and Saul was being trained to walk by words and not by a vision, which is the precursor to walking by faith. *For faith comes by hearing and hearing by the word of God*. **(Romans 10:17)** God was training his ears so that when he got back his sight, he wouldn't focus on what he saw; he'd focus on what God said.

⁸ "Hearing the voice but seeing no one. So Saul got up from the ground, but though his eyes were open he could see nothing."

God took away his natural eyes to develop his spiritual eyes. We have some people with good natural eyes who can't see spiritually. My friends, you cannot allow others' vision or lack thereof to blur or derail your vision. Only Saul could see what Jesus had for him to do. You receive on the level you believe.

Saul got up from the ground, but though his eyes were open, he could not see, so they led him by hand. This goes in line with Psalms 37:23, which says, *"The steps of a good man are ordered by the Lord."* Saul had to follow the voice of others. He had to relinquish control and had to submit himself to be a follower. To be a great leader, you must be a great follower first.

⁹ But though his eyes were open he could not see so they led him by hand and brought him to Damascus and he was unable to see for three days.

Three is a significant number when it comes to transformation. Jesus spent three days in a tomb. Jonah spent three days in the belly of the whale. And Saul spent three days blind. The number three connects to the Holy Trinity: Father, Son, and Holy Spirit. And they work in concert when it comes to creating a new thing. God was transforming him from Saul to Paul.

10 Now in Damascus there was a disciple named Ananias; and <u>**the Lord said to him in a vision**</u>**, "Ananias." And he answered, "Here I am, Lord."**

We see here God speaks through what? A vision.

"And Ananias, and he answered, "Here I am Lord...Here I am Lord."

Ananias moved swiftly. At the beginning of the verse, we hear the word 'disciple.' A disciple is a disciplined one. For God to call him a disciple implies that God had already marked him and called him for service in the kingdom. We often don't move as quickly as we should because we don't know the voice of God. Ananias must have already experienced and learned the voice of God. God knew who to call when He needed a messenger. And our goal should be to stay ready and in a position that when God calls, we answer, "Here I am, Lord."

How many times has God spoken to you in a vision, and you couldn't figure out it was Him?

I know I have not always received and understood the visions in my life. My goal is always to get better, so don't be discouraged if you don't get every vision from God correctly. It is vital that we understand the importance of obedience to God's voice because lives are attached to us following God's voice. We can all be receivers and messengers of God and must ensure our hearing devices are working properly. We don't want to be the reason why a kingdom agenda is stalled.

11 *And the Lord said to him, "Get up and go to the street called Straight, and ask at the house of Judas for a man from Tarsus named Saul; for he is praying [there],*

Saul, though he was blind, was still able to pray. Before this, we had never heard of a man named Saul who *prayed*. We heard of a Saul who *preyed* on Christians. When you are obedient to God's vision, He will take you from preying to praying! Something about when you can't see anything makes you start praying. As he was praying, the Bible says God spoke to Ananias and said there was a man praying right then.

As Saul was praying and communicating with God, God sent Ananias to go get him. You will notice here that God used Saul's prayer to communicate with him regarding Ananias meeting him. We can learn from this that when our vision is limited, God will give us spiritual vision through our prayers. Isaiah 65:24 gives us an example of God moving through prayers.

Isaiah 65:24 (NLT)
I will answer them before they even call to me. While they are still talking about their needs, I will go ahead and answer their prayers!

Okay, back to Acts 9

12 and in a vision he has seen a man named Ananias come in and place his hands on him, so that he may regain his sight."

Ananias gets a vision that Paul is praying, and then Paul gets a vision that Ananias is coming. If you're a note taker, God gives the revelation in the vision. In the meeting (between Saul and Ananias) is a manifestation. After the meeting, he had confirmation. I'm going to say that again. God will give you the revelation in the vision. Then, He caused manifestation with a meeting. With the meeting comes total confirmation. So, when I get the vision, I'm waiting to see some manifestation; after manifestation, I can truly identify and confirm if it's God. In a vision, Saul has seen a man named Ananias come in and place his hands on him so that he may regain sight.

I'm jumping to Acts 9:17

17 So Ananias left and entered the house, and he laid his hands on Saul and said, "Brother Saul, the Lord Jesus, who appeared to you on the road as you came [to Damascus], has sent me so that you may regain your sight and be filled with the Holy Spirit [in order to proclaim Christ to both Jews and Gentiles]." 18 Immediately something like scales fell from Saul's eyes, and he regained his sight. Then he got up and was baptized; 19 and he took some food and was strengthened.

Ananias references the vision to Saul as confirmation of something he should not have known. When a person comes and tells you about a vision they shouldn't know, we call that confirmation. The confirmation gives you peace that the person could be a trusted source.

Wisdom Key: God reveals Himself in visions

Numbers 12:6 (AMP)

6 And He said, "Hear now My words: If there is a prophet among you, I the Lord will make Myself known to him in a vision And I will speak to him in a dream.

God showed me a vision of thousands of people when we were not in ministry, and it has occurred.

God predicts our future in visions.

In Habakkuk 2, look what it says:
And I will stand at my guard post and station myself on the tower and I will keep watch to see what he will say to me and what answer I will give as a spokesman when I am reproved. Then the Lord answered me and said: Write the vision and engrave it plainly on clay tablets so that the one who reads it will run. For the vision is yet for an appointed future time, it hurries towards the goal of fulfillment. It will not fail even though it delays, wait patient for it because it will certainly come, it will not delay.

It is critical you write down visions. We paid a deposit for plans for the new building, and we were only in our current building for eight months. The vision should always be on the next—the next goal, the next plan, and the next level.

During our process, the pandemic hit, construction backlogs, light pole issues, and our project got delayed. And we had to sit there, look at dirt, and be uncomfortable for this season. But it was the vision that kept us going. That's why the Bible says without a vision, the people perish, and without revelation, people get weary. It is so critical to have the vision to keep you going. It is mentioned in **Hebrews 12:2** that the vision set before Jesus helped Him endure the cross. Even Jesus had to have the vision to help Him. How much more do we need to have a vision? Remember, every vision will have setbacks, roadblocks, and adversarial challenges. But if you can stay the course, what God gave you in a vision will manifest in the natural realm. The truth is, we all will be on our own road to Damascus at some point in life. We will have two choices: either walk by sight and base our hopes on what we see or be led by the vision that God gave us to help us get through the tough seasons. Tough times don't last; tough people do!

You are responsible for writing the vision He gives you. He then says, *"Though it tarry, wait for it, it's going to surely come to pass."* You may say that I'm crazy, and I'm fine with that. Most successful people are considered crazy at some point in their lives. If you go into my office, I have plans everywhere, and even though we're in this building, I'm planning for the next building. Even though you're in this house, there's nothing wrong with going to look at a new house. Even though you're in a car, there's nothing wrong with looking at something new, and it doesn't cost anything to test drive it.

Once I was diagnosed with cancer, I really had some tough questions that I wanted God to answer. Now, we know from the story of Job that God doesn't have to answer any questions from us. God has total sovereignty over our lives, but I still wanted to know why I had to go through the season of cancer. So, one day, when I went in to get a PET scan, I remember asking God why again. As I lay down on the table and it moved into the tube to scan my body, I saw a vision, and I heard a voice. The voice said that if I kept my hands up, it would be alright. At that moment, I had instant peace. God had answered my question. Though I was going through this season, God was going to bring me through if I surrendered it all to Him. I don't know who needs this word right now, but you may be going through something too difficult to carry. I want you right now to give it to God. Release it. As **1 Peter 7** tells us.

1 Peter 5:7 says to cast all your cares upon the Lord who cares for you.

We all have a choice: we can carry our burden, or we can cast our burden. The choice is yours. Choose to cast your burden upon the Lord today.

Questions

1. What is the difference between a vision and a dream to you?

2. How do you fight spiritually?

3. Have you ever had a Damascus Road experience?

4. Why do you think God took Saul's sight?

5. Why do you think Jesus engaged in this situation?

6. Do you think you are a better seer than a listener?

7. Do you allow what you see to affect what you hear?

8. How can we train ourselves to be better listeners?

9. Has God ever told you to move on with something giving you clarity?

10. Name a time in your life when you walked by faith, not sight.

11. Has God ever given you confirmation on one of your visions? And how did He confirm it?

Chapter Nine

Dreams

Dreams are a natural part of the human experience, varying from scary to action-packed and to some being of a sexual nature. They are often so real it wakes us out of our sleep in a sweat. I know for me, the scariest dreams are me falling from a high place.

As I studied dreams, God gave me some fresh revelation on hearing through them. I read, "Dreams are the perfect way to hear from God. When you're dreaming, you are quiet."

Could it be that God doesn't talk because *you* talk too much?

Do you have a one-sided relationship with God?

Have you thought about just being quiet and allowing God time to connect with you?

God chooses to give you revelation while you are sleeping. You're quiet, so you can't ignore Him and have no distractions. You're basically all ears for the time you sleep. It's been said we have two ears and one mouth. Therefore, we should listen twice as much as we speak.

Let's look at **Acts 2:17**, which says: *"It shall be in the last days, says God, that I will pour out my Spirit upon all mankind and* *your son and your daughter shall prophesy, and your young men shall see divinely <u>prompted</u> visions, and your old men shall dream divinely prompted dreams."*

The word 'prompted' means to clue in or to initiate. God gives you these prompts for us to pay attention, to say, **"Check this out!"** or **"Be mindful!"** In these dreams, we often wake up wondering if God is trying to talk to us.

Let's go to the book of Job.

Job 33:14-19 (AMP)

[14] *"For God speaks once, And even twice, yet no one notices it [including you, Job].* [15] *"In a dream, a vision of the night [one may hear God's voice], <u>When deep sleep falls on men While slumbering upon the bed,</u>* [16] *<u>Then He opens the ears of men And seals their instruction,</u>*

God says through Elihu, " **I'm talking to you but you don't even notice it."** *In a dream, a vision of night one may hear God's voice.* You see it? Then it says, **"When deep sleep falls on men while slumbering upon the bed then he opens the ears of men."**

Wait a second, why does He have to wait for you to sleep to open your ears?

Why couldn't your ears be open from the beginning?

At times, God must get us asleep so we can listen. It didn't say little sleep; it said deep sleep. Look at what it says: **"And he opens the ears of men and seals their instruction."**

I have read that many wealthy people sleep with something they can write on near their bed. Some of the best ideas will drop in while we sleep.

Look what **Job 33:17** says:

17 That He may turn man aside from his conduct, And keep him from pride; 18 He holds back his soul from the pit [of destruction], And his life from passing over into Sheol (the nether world, the place of the dead).

God will use dreams as a warning to help you change course. When we can't hear Him through other means, He'll try to connect to us through our dreams to tap into our subconscious. Our responsibility is to capture and lock in on the thoughts that God has for us. For those of you who may be wrestling with obedience to something, God has dropped into your spirit through a dream.

Here are 8 indicators that have helped me in the past to determine if my dream was a message from God.

1. **It lines up with the word of God**. God will never go against His word. He's holy, meaning everything lines up. *"All Scripture is given by inspiration of God, and is profitable for doctrine, for reproof, for correction, for instruction in righteousness, that the man of God may be complete, thoroughly equipped for every good work" (II Timothy 3:16-17).*

2. **It will speak to our heart**: *"For this is the covenant that I will make with the house of Israel after those days, says the Lord: I will put my laws into their minds, and I will write them on their hearts. and I will be their God, and they shall be my people. And they shall not teach everyone his fellow citizen, and everyone his brother, saying, 'know the Lord,' for all will know Me, from the least to the greatest of them"* (Hebrews 8:10-11).

3. **It will be followed up with Godly counsel**: God will have people who have the wisdom to speak into your life to confirm or nudge you in the right direction. *"Where no counsel is, the people fall: but in the multitude of counselors there is safety"* (Proverbs 11:14)

4. **It will challenge your faith.** God calls us to Faith, and, ultimately, faith will take us out of our comfort zone. **Hebrews 11:6** says *it is impossible to please God without faith for those who come to God must first believe he exists and believe that he is a rewarder of those who diligently*

seek Him. We can deduce that if we are not in faith for something, we are not in a position to please God.

5. **It comes with confirmation:** *"By the mouth of two or three witnesses every fact may be confirmed"* (Matthew 18:16).

6. **It comes with The Prophetic (word of knowledge, word of wisdom, personal prophecy):** *"Do not quench the Spirit; do not despise prophetic utterances. But examine everything carefully; hold fast to that which is good"* (1 Thessalonians 5:19-21).

7. **It comes with peace in your heart:** *"Let the peace of Christ rule in your hearts, to which indeed you were called in one body; and be thankful"* (Colossians 3:15).

8. **It lines up with circumstances/timing:** *"After these things he (Paul) left Athens and went to Corinth. And he found a certain Jew named Aquila, a native of Pontus, having recently come from Italy with his wife Priscilla, because Claudius had commanded all the Jews to leave Rome. He came to them, and because he was of the same trade, he stayed with them and they were working; for by trade they were tent-makers"* (**Acts 18:1-3** -- this relationship between Paul, Aquila and Priscilla -- which happened as a result of circumstances -- became one of the most important strategic partnerships in the book of Acts).

When I'm in a place of confusion, I go to **Matthew 7:7-9** and **Jer. 33:3** to help me navigate through my decision-making process.

Matthew 7:7-9 (AMP)

⁷ "Ask and keep on asking and it will be given to you; seek and keep on seeking and you will find; knock and keep on knocking and the door will be opened to you. 8 For everyone who keeps on asking receives, and he who keeps on seeking finds, and to him who keeps on knocking, it will be opened.

Jeremiah 33:3 (AMP)

³ 'Call to Me and I will answer you, and tell you [and even show you] great and mighty things, [things which have been confined and hidden], which you do not know and understand and cannot distinguish.'

For those of you who may be in the valley of decision, it's a time to ask serious questions and reach out to others that have been where you want to go.

Wisdom Keys

Number One: God uses dreams to warn us

Matthew 2:11 says: *¹¹And after entering the house, they saw the Child with Mary His mother; and they fell down and* *worshiped Him. Then, after opening their treasure chests, they presented to Him gifts [fit for a king, gifts] of gold, frankincense, and myrrh. ¹² And having been warned [by God] in a dream not to go back to Herod, the magi left for their own country by another way.*

God warns you not to do certain things in dreams. Now let me be clear, not every dream is from God. "**Now, Pastor, how do I tell the difference between a God dream and a devil dream?**"

Any dream that is leading you to sin is not of God! Whatever God gives you will line up with His word.

God tried to warn King Nebuchadnezzar through a dream in the book of Daniel.

Daniel 2:1, *"In the second year of the reign of Nebuchadnezzar, Nebuchadnezzar had dreams which troubled and disturbed his spirit..."* The dreams interfered with his ability to sleep. We must assume that the king had all his needs met, yet he could not sleep. An inability to sleep soundly could be an indicator that you need to set an appointment with God. The promise of God is sweet sleep **(Proverbs 3:24)**.

Number Two: God uses dreams to help us from poor decisions

Matthew 27:19 (AMP)

"Just then as Pilate was sitting on the judgment seat, his wife sent him a message, "Leave that innocent man alive. I have suffered through a terrible nightmare about him last night."

Family, please give credence to those who are close to you when they dream about you. God might be trying to talk to you through them. I've learned the Holy Spirit sounds a lot like our spouses!

Do I have any witnesses?

And that's why we have a problem listening. Pilate's wife said to leave Jesus alone, and that stopped Pilate from having Jesus's blood on His hands directly. When I get a word or message, I am unsure about, I don't just dismiss it. The Bible says to test the Spirit, so I take it to the Lord in prayer and say, **"Lord is this you?"**

I remember when we lived in Orlando, and I was speaking at a school for the FCAT pep rally. I was debating whether speaking was my gift. The next day I was at the community pool swimming, and a young boy came and said, **"Are you Jomo Cousins?"**

I said, **"Yeah..."**

He said, **"Thank you for what you said at school this week."**

As he was talking, all I could think of was **Hebrews 13:2 – "Be mindful you may be entertaining angels unawares."**

God will drop people in your life to give you a word. The challenge is we dismiss a message because of the messenger. Forget the messenger and focus on the message. We dismiss people because we don't like the way they're packaged. Remember, God can use anyone at any time.

Number Three: God uses dreams to confirm things for us

Genesis 28:10-12 (AMP)

10 Now Jacob left Beersheba [never to see his mother again] and traveled toward Haran. 11 And he came to a certain place and stayed overnight there because the sun had set. Taking one of the stones of the place, he put it under his head and lay down there [to sleep]. 12 He dreamed that there was a ladder (stairway) placed on the earth, and the top of it reached [out of sight] toward heaven; and [he saw] the angels of God ascending and descending on it [going to and from heaven]. "And behold the Lord stood above... around him said "I am the Lord God, the God of Abraham your father's Father and the God of Isaac. I will give to you and to your descendants the land of promise of which your line, your descendants...say shall be countless as the dust of the earth and you shall spread abroad to the West, the East and the North and the South and all your families..."

Jacob was anxious about his journey home, for he left like a theft in the night. And now he's heading home thinking about his brother Esau's revenge. God gave him peace amid despair in a dream.

In this dream, God gave Jacob a vision of how the prayer chain works. Jacob saw what looked like a ladder leading to heaven. Imagine a stairway placed on earth and the top reached heaven. As we start praying, angels start going up, and it is at that moment some of the prayers you've been praying for are coming down.

Number Four: God uses dreams to give you a sense of urgency

Genesis 41:32 (AMP)

"That the dream was repeated twice to Pharaoh and in two different ways indicates that the matter is fully determined and established by God, and God will bring it to pass very quickly."

Isn't that good? Us having repeated dreams about the same thing is an indication that it's settled and it's going to happen quickly.

So what have you been dreaming about? When God's going to transition you, He'll often give you a dream. Write it down so that when it starts to happen, you'll have the peace that is God.

Number 5: God uses dreams to provide revelation

Daniel 7:1, look what it says:

⁷ In the first year of Belshazzar king of Babylon Daniel had a dream and visions appeared in his mind as he lay on his bed; then <u>he wrote the dream down</u> and related a summary of it.

The first thing he did after the dream was to write it down. I wanted to emphasize this because it's through us writing things down that we develop the pattern by which God speaks to us. God communicates in the manner that is best for each child. I would start to journal how and when God answers. By doing this, you will build your faith in God's ability, which will help you to see how God moves in your life, and you can catalog your faith.

For example, "**I prayed for this, and God answered with this. I prayed for that, and God answered with that.**"

And as you do this, you will start to see God's hands all over your life. So when the next faith fight comes, you can say, "**You know what, God did it once, and He can do it again.**"

Number Six: Dreams bring peace

Matthew 1:20 (AMP)

"But after he considered this the angel of the Lord appeared in a dream saying, "Joseph the son of David, <u>do not be afraid to take Mary as your wife for the child who has been conceived in her is of the Holy Spirit.</u>"

Now, this is a tough one. I don't know if I could have done this. Your fiancé claims to be a virgin, but she's pregnant. It was so rough on Joseph that God said, **"I got to talk to him."** God gave Joseph peace through a dream to marry her.

My goal is for you to not minimize your dreams any longer and really start to tap into **"is it God speaking to me?"**

When a dream comes, here are the four things you need to do.

1. **Pray.** Before you do anything else, pray that God exposes the source of the dream and what He wants to teach you through it. Pray, **"Lord, what does this mean? Lord, what are you trying to tell me?" James 1:5 says anyone who lacks wisdom should ask God, for He'll give it to you liberally.**

2. **Listen to God.** Take a moment to sit quietly before the Lord and ask Him, **"Lord, what do you want me to do with this?"** Once you feel peace about the direction, then move with it. No peace, you're not in it. Peace is one of the key indicators that you're in the will. When you're not at peace, you must do something.

3. **Write it down**. I already told you that. Get a notebook. Notebook says, "**When God speaks**." What I do is when someone is further along than me in the faith walk, and I trust their walk, I write down what they say to me, so I don't forget it.

4. **Seek Godly counsel**. When I reference seeking Godly counsel, find people who have walked the path you want and have survived. It could be a pastor. It could be a brother/sister or father/mother. It should be someone with evidence of a Godly walk who can speak into your life.

Questions

1. Has God ever spoken to you in a dream?

2. Do you have a one-sided relationship with God? Or do you give Him space to speak to you?

3. What is a prompt?

4. And how does God prompt you?

5. Have you ever acted on a dream?

6. Have you ever acted on a dream, and you were wrong?

7. What are the indicators of a dream being from God?

8. What scriptures should we use when asking God?

9. What are some things God communicates to us in dreams?

10. What are the things you need to do after you have a dream that you believe is from God?

Chapter Ten

Know Thy Enemy

When I was a kid, my favorite cartoon was *GI Joe*. *GI Joe* was a cartoon show about the military. I loved the characters and the constant battle between the good and bad guys. GI Joe had a famous statement: "knowing is half the battle." The prophet Hosea said a similar statement in his book: ***"my people are destroyed for lack of knowledge."* (Hosea 4:6)**

Knowing how to hear from God is one of the most critical aspects of our faith walk. We miss God's messages because we haven't spent the time to discern His voice. As I was preparing this chapter, "Know Thy Enemy," I realized that one of the major challenges for many people is that they have trouble knowing whose voice they hear. Logically, if we believe in a God who speaks, we also must believe in an enemy who speaks.

My goal is to teach you how to identify the voice of the enemy. If you can identify his voice, then it will help you make better decisions. When I thought of writing about this, I was studying counterfeits and copies. They say the best way to spot a counterfeit is to study the original. Did you know the Secret Service was instituted to deal with counterfeiting? It was never about security! It was all about making sure they could identify the real thing.

Bankers or those in the currency industry are people who study money constantly. Their study of money consists of learning the distinguishing qualities of the original. And based on this study, they can quickly discern if something is a counterfeit. So, when a person says, "Jomo, I don't know if it's God's voice or not," it may be that you or they haven't studied the original enough or have not invested enough time in His word to know His voice.

In this chapter, we're going to be focusing on **Genesis 3**. In **Genesis 3**, the devil comes into the garden and starts a conversation with Eve.

Genesis 3 (AMP)

¹ Now the serpent was more crafty (subtle, skilled in deceit) than any living creature of the field which the Lord God had made. And the serpent (Satan) said to the woman, <u>"Can it really be that God has said, 'You shall not eat from any tree of the garden'?"</u> ² And the woman said to the serpent, "We may eat fruit from the trees of the garden, ³ <u>except the fruit from the tree which is in the middle of the garden. God said, 'You shall not eat from it nor touch it, otherwise you will die.'"</u> ⁴ But the serpent said to the woman, <u>"You certainly will not die! ⁵ For God knows that on the day you eat from it your eyes will be opened [that is, you will have greater awareness], and you will be like God, knowing [the difference between] good and evil."</u> ⁶ And when the woman saw that the tree was good for food, and that it was delightful to look at, and a tree to be desired in order to make one wise and insightful, she took some of its fruit and ate it; and she also gave some to her husband with her, and *he ate. ⁷ Then the eyes of the two of them were opened [that is, their awareness increased], and they knew that they were naked; and they fastened fig leaves together and made themselves coverings.*

In these verses, the devil uses a little truth with every statement to trick them. When you study the devil's words used in this passage, you will notice that 46% of what he said is true. The devil planted a seed of doubt that God was holding something back from them. Since God gave us free will and the opportunity to choose our path, we are often led astray by our lust for more. They fell for the scheme because they didn't trust that God had their best interest at heart.

We are so preoccupied with our "next" that we don't appreciate our "now." We must understand how the devil works. So Let's read. **John 8:44 (AMP)**

"You are of your father the devil and it's your will to practice the desires which are characteristic of your father. He was a murderer from the beginning and does not stand in the truth because there is no truth in him. When he lies he speaks what is natural for him for he's a liar and the father of lies, and half-truths.

Every time you lie, you're acting like the devil. He is the father of lies. God wants you hot or cold, not lukewarm **(Rev. 3:16)**. I have a real issue with lying and try my best not to do it. There was a time when people would call the house and ask, "**Can I** *talk to Charmaine?*" I would say she was asleep when she wasn't because I was trying to protect her from people that drained her. I wanted her to get some rest. But once I understood the ramifications of the small lies inducing larger ones, I decided to deal in truth, even if I must hurt someone's feelings. I now say, "**She is wide awake and doesn't want to talk to you right now!** "We must deal in truth.

I want to drill down on this point. If our goal is to hear God's voice clearly but constantly lie, we are flowing on the wrong frequency to hear God. We can't practice sin and expect to hear God, who is truth.

It's difficult to consistently do this when you want to avoid conflict. I don't know if you have ever been trapped in a question with no good answer.

(example): "**How do I look in this dress?**" And you tell the truth: "**I don't like it.**"

"Hey, babe, I really don't like it." **Deal in truth...** See, if you don't deal in truth, they will eventually wear that outfit again. Because you said you liked it but didn't like it, now we have a problem. No, deal in what? "**Truth.**"

When my wife wears something I really like, I will lavish her with praise because that's the truth. I say, "**Girl, you look good. Glory to God, You're my good thing. You look good.**" She knows when I speak to her, I'm speaking to her in truth. Therefore, when I say I don't like something, she can accept it because she knows that I deal in truth, whether good or bad. If you don't build your life on truth, how will anybody ever know when you are telling the truth? People will respect and honor you when you deal in truth.

Genesis 3:2 *"And the woman said to the serpent, "We may eat from the trees of the garden, except the fruit of the tree which is in the middle of the garden." ³ except the fruit from the tree which is in the middle of the garden. God said, 'You shall not eat from it nor touch it, otherwise you will die.'" ⁴ But the serpent said to the woman, "You certainly will not die!*

Understand that she not only heard it but also knew the consequences of her actions. Your life is based on your choices, your decisions, and your consequences. We all have a choice, we all must decide, but the consequences are outside of our control. In this passage, God was clear about the ramifications of disobedience; it said '*die*.' The challenge is she did not understand the first death was spiritual death, meaning separation from the Father, and the second death would be a natural death, which would happen in time. They didn't have the revelation and knowledge to know what they were getting themselves into. Be careful who you talk to; they may be deeper than you. The devil had a greater understanding of things of God than they did.

⁵ For God knows that on the day you eat from it your eyes will be opened [that is, you will have greater awareness], and you

will be like God, knowing [the difference between] good and evil."

As parents, we try to prevent our children from making the same mistakes that we did, but for some reason, they must find out on their own. I wonder if anyone else has children similar to mine? What is it in our nature that makes us disobey? Why? We think we know it all. The root of it is pride.

People will say, "***I know better; my way is better; it was a different time when you were growing up; I got this.***"

Now, God's been here from the beginning, and He has given you a book with all the clues, and you're trying to play the game without the book—it doesn't make much sense to me. When I was in the NFL, they gave us a big playbook with all the plays. They don't have a playbook now; instead, they give you an electronic tablet. In it, you have all these plays, and before the game on Saturday nights, they'd give us a quiz to see if we knew where we were supposed to be on a given play. Poor performance on this quiz was an indicator that you were not ready to play the game.

If God gave you a quiz today, could He put you in the game? Would you know your playbook? During the week leading up to the game, they would give us keys to victory. They would give us all the tendencies of our opponents, so we would be prepared for different situations that may arise. On every down of a football game, they gave us statistics so that we could make winning plays. Then, when we got into the game, we already knew what our opponents thought because we had studied them. *Know thy enemy.*

So, do you know your enemy? He's the author of lies. His goal is always to give you a shortcut, to lie your way out of something.

I remember going to the mall one time when I was in New Jersey and didn't have real money. A guy opened his jacket up and said, "**What do you want?**" Anybody bought some stolen or fake jewelry, and you thought you got to a deal? Man, you had a rash around your neck so big. It looked like gold. I thought I got a Rolex. I should say I got a *Rolax* because that thing stopped immediately. The devil is the master of giving you a shortcut masked in blessing or breakthrough.

The devil is always trying to replace God. Therefore, he is always trying to find ways to get in your ear because we know that faith comes by hearing **Romans 10:17.**

Isaiah 14 shows us the devil's plan.

Isaiah 14:12 (AMP)

"How you have fallen from heaven, O star of the morning [light-bringer], son of the dawn! You have been cut down to the ground, You who have weakened the nations [king of Babylon]!
¹³ "But you said in your heart,
'I will ascend to heaven;

I will raise my throne above the stars of God;
I will sit on the mount of assembly
In the remote parts of the north.
¹⁴ *'I will ascend above the heights of the clouds;*
I will make myself like the Most High.'

The devil's job was to bring light and worship to God. But he got caught up in pride. You will notice there were many *I will's* in the verses we read. Brothers and sisters, you must be very mindful of how the enemy works because his goal is to get you double-minded. Remember, the Bible says, "**A double-minded man is unstable in all his ways.**" (James 1:8)

When Adam and Eve were just listening to God, there was only one voice by which they had to respond to and receive. But, when they opened themselves up to the devil, they had to discern whose voice it was. This is the epitome of being double-minded. With one voice, there is no choice but with multiple voices come multiple choices. His goal is to get you to where you make the wrong decision or fall into indecision. I want you to understand, my friends, that indecision is a decision. It's just a slow no. Our lack of action can be traced back to us not comprehending God's voice. And with that lack of action, you have now fallen into disobedience.

Let's go back to Genesis 3. Look what it says:

⁶ *And when the woman saw that the tree was good for food, and that it was delightful to look at, and a tree to be desired*

in order to make one wise and insightful, she took some of its fruit and ate it; and she also gave some to her husband with her, and he ate. ⁷ Then the eyes of the two of them were opened [that is, their awareness increased], and they knew that they were naked; and they fastened fig leaves together and made themselves coverings.

Eve believed the enemy's report. It seems that when people fall, they bring somebody with them.

⁸ And they heard the sound of the Lord God walking in the garden in the cool [afternoon breeze] of the day, so the man and his wife hid and kept themselves hidden from the presence of the Lord God among the trees of the garden. ⁹ But the Lord God called to Adam, and said to him, "Where are you?" ¹⁰ He said, "I heard the sound of You [walking] in the garden, and I was afraid because I was naked; so I hid myself." ¹¹ God said, "Who told you that you were naked? Have you eaten [fruit] from the tree of which I commanded you not to eat?" 12 And the man said, "The woman whom You gave to be with me—she gave me [fruit] from the tree, and I ate it." ¹³ Then the Lord God said to the woman, "What is this that you have done?" And the woman said, "The serpent beguiled and deceived me, and I ate [from the forbidden tree]."

Adam and Eve's problem was they didn't take God at his word. It wasn't that they didn't know. It was that they did not trust God's voice. Jesus said, **"You do not believe me, you do not trust and follow me because you are not my sheep. The sheep that are my own hear my voice, listen to me, I know them and** *they follow me."* (John 10:27)

If we are constantly lying, we are taking on the devil's character. We can't follow God and follow the devil at the same time. As a result, you must ask yourself, *"**Who am I following?**"*

Wisdom Keys:

Number One: We must know who we are

Matthew 4:1-3 (AMP)

The Temptation of Jesus
[1] Then Jesus was led by the [Holy] Spirit into the wilderness to be tempted by the devil. [2] After He had gone without food for forty days and forty nights, He became hungry. [3] And the tempter came and said to Him, "If You are the Son of God, command that these stones become bread."

The devil came after Adam and Eve with questions about what God said to them. Now, look at how he comes at Jesus. You will hear his voice clearly when you're hungry, thirsty, or lonely. Notice after he had gone without food for 40 days, the tempter came. When you're on the verge of a breakthrough, the devil seems to show up with a shortcut.

My wife and I were offered a job at a large ministry before we started the church. The offer was very enticing. They asked me if I wanted a Mercedes S600 or Cadillac Escalade. They offered me a nice base salary, and we would have armor bearers as the proverbial icing on the cake.

I said, "**My God!**" I was excited about the opportunity.

During this time, I was in the process of deliberating this opportunity. I was not sure God was telling me to start a church. I had to decide: Do I preach to 5,000 people to start off with it, or do I start a church with my family in a building with no air conditioning?

It seems like an easy decision, but the Holy Spirit said, **"Jomo, you start with nothing."**

I said, "**No, Lord, no!**"

Please don't judge me, I have always been a provider for my family, and I never wanted to be in a position where I couldn't provide for my wife and kids. Financial stability was high on my list. At the time, I just couldn't see how a church could provide. I know it seems like an easy decision now, but it wasn't then. I thought to myself, If I started off in a large successful church, my life would be easier.

When I was in that space (valley of decision), I prayed, and God confirmed the same message: "**start a church with nothing but Me.**" The message came to me in a dream and blew my mind. The pastor of the church I was considering had a knife at my neck in a threatening manner. I woke up the next day with clarity that this was not the place for me.

I interpreted the dream as my taking this job being the death of my speaking gift. And my wife confirmed it, saying, *"**Jomo can you handle that environment? Because you are going to say something that will get you fired!**"* I have always had the ability to say what needs to be said to people who don't want to hear it. I said, *"**you're right, I will say something to get me fired.**"*

Number Two: Don't be led by your natural needs

Matthew 4:4 (AMP)

⁴ But Jesus replied, "It is written and forever remains written, 'Man shall not live by bread alone, but by every word that comes out of the mouth of God.'"

The only way the devil can win is if we lack knowledge of God's word. Jesus's flesh wanted the bread, but His Spirit stood on the Word. The tempter always comes with food first, much as he did in Genesis when he came with the fruit. The enemy comes with food first, for it's an essential need for survival.

*"**If you're the son of God, command these stones to become bread.**"* The enemy will come at you with a natural need in order for you to break a spiritual promise. We all must eat, but if the meal leads to disobedience, it's not worth it. *It is a natural need, but it's not a new need.*

Keys to discerning the voice of the enemy:

- **He will always have you question your identity.**
- **He will offer you a shortcut.**
- **He will conflict with God's word.**
- **He will sow seeds of doubt.**
- **He will try to confuse you with words.**

Questions

1. Can you name a time when the devil spoke to you?

2. What was he asking you to do?

3. What are some keys that you need to know that it's not God talking to you?

4. Has anybody ever had you question God's word?

5. Have you ever lied to not hurt someone's feelings?

6. Do you struggle with consistently telling the truth?

7. Do you know someone who always lies? What do you think about that person?

8. How did the devil trick them?

9. What can we do to not fall into the same trap?

10. Have you ever made a bad decision that affected others?

11. In what areas does the devil consistently test you?

Made in the USA
Monee, IL
19 November 2022

18090099R00098